The Russian Federation

Denial of justice

Amnesty International is a worldwide voluntary activist movement working for human rights. It is independent of any government, political persuasion or religious creed. It does not support or oppose any government or political system, nor does it support or oppose the views of those whose rights it seeks to protect. It is concerned solely with the impartial protection of human rights.

Amnesty International's vision is of a world in which every person enjoys all the human rights enshrined in the Universal Declaration of Human Rights and other international human rights standards.

Amnesty International undertakes research and action focused on preventing and ending grave abuses of the rights to physical and mental integrity, freedom of conscience and expression, and freedom from discrimination. In this context, it:

- seeks the release of prisoners of conscience: these are people detained for their political, religious or other conscientiously held beliefs or because of their ethnic origin, sex, colour, language, national or social origin, economic status, birth or other status – who have not used or advocated violence;
- works for fair and prompt trials for all political prisoners;
- opposes without reservation the death penalty, torture and other cruel, inhuman or degrading treatment or punishment;
- campaigns for an end to political killings and "disappearances";
- calls on governments to refrain from unlawful killings in armed conflict;
- calls on armed political groups to end abuses such as the detention of prisoners of conscience, hostage-taking, torture and unlawful killings;
- opposes abuses by non-state actors where the state has failed to fulfil its obligations to provide effective protection;
- campaigns for perpetrators of human rights abuses to be brought to justice;
- seeks to assist asylum-seekers who are at risk of being returned to a country where they might suffer serious abuses of their human rights;
- opposes certain grave abuses of economic, social and cultural rights.

Amnesty International also seeks to:

- cooperate with other non-governmental organizations, the United Nations and regional intergovernmental organizations;
- ensure control of international military, security and police relations to prevent human rights abuses;
- organize human rights education and awareness raising programs.

Amnesty International is a democratic, self-governing movement with more than a million members and supporters in over 140 countries and territories. It is funded largely by its worldwide membership and public donations.

The Russian Federation

Denial of justice

Amnesty International Publications

Please note that readers may find some of the photographs and case histories contained in this report disturbing.

First published in 2002 by
Amnesty International Publications
International Secretariat
Peter Benenson House
1 Easton Street
London WC1X oDW
United Kingdom

www.amnesty.org

© Copyright
Amnesty International Publications 2002
ISBN: 0-86210-318-5
AI Index: EUR 46/027/2002
Original language: English

Printed by:
The Alden Press
Osney Mead
Oxford
United Kingdom

CONTENTS

Glossary

amnesty   a provision sanctioned by parliament for a limited period that provides for the release of convicted prisoners. In previous amnesties, those convicted of crimes carrying prison sentences of less than six years have been freed. Those convicted of qualifying offences during the amnesty period are eligible for release in the courtroom upon sentencing.

CC   Criminal Code (*Ugolovnyi kodeks*)

CEDAW   Committee on the Elimination of Discrimination against Women

Convention against Torture
    UN Convention against Torture and Other Cruel, Inhuman or Degrading Treatment or Punishment

CPC   Criminal Procedure Code (*Ugolovno protsessual'nyi kodeks*)

CPT   European Committee for the Prevention of Torture and Inhuman or Degrading Treatment or Punishment

CRC   UN Convention on the Rights of the Child

ECHR   European Convention for the Protection of Human Rights and Fundamental Freedoms

FSB   *Federalnaia sluzhba bezopasnosti* (the federal security service)

Geneva Conventions
    The four Geneva Conventions of 1949 and their two Additional Protocols of 1977 are the principal instruments of international humanitarian law, also known as the laws of war. International humanitarian law is the body of rules and principles which seeks to protect those who are not participating in the hostilities, including combatants who are wounded or captured, by limiting the means and methods of conducting military operations. Its central purpose is to limit and prevent human suffering in times of armed conflict. The rules are to be observed not only by governments and their armed forces, but also by

	armed political groups and any other parties to a conflict. The Russian Federation is a party to the Geneva Conventions and their Additional Protocols.
KGB	*Komitet gosudarstvennoi bezopasnosti* (the former state security service)
ICCPR	International Covenant on Civil and Political Rights
MSP	Military, security and police transfers
OMON	*Otriad militsii osobogo naznacheniia* (special police detachments or riot police)
OSCE	Organization for Security and Co-operation in Europe
procuracy	the official state body responsible for conducting criminal investigations (*prokuratura*)
procurator	an employee of the procuracy responsible for investigating crimes and prosecuting them in court (*prokuror*)
RUBOP	*Regional'noe upravlenie po bor'be s organizovannoi prestupnost'iu* (literally, the Regional Department on fighting Organized Crime, or Organized Crime Squad), a law enforcement agency
SIZO	*Sledstvennyi izoliator* (pre-trial detention facility)
"Spetsnaz"	literally, "special purpose" units that can refer to special units of armed forces or the police force, such as those deployed in prison riots
UNHCR	United Nations High Commissioner for Refugees
USSR	Union of Soviet Socialist Republics, or Soviet Union, dissolved in 1991
VOVD	*Vremennoe otdelenie vnutrennikh del* (literally, Temporary Department of Internal Affairs; temporary police station)

Transliteration system

Amnesty International has adopted a modified version of the US Library of Congress transliteration system for Russian names and words written in English. Exceptions include names for which there is an internationally recognized representation in English or where a Russian organization has chosen to represent itself in English according to a specific spelling. This system is not intended to be a guide to pronunciation.

ДЕТИ
РОССИИ ЗА
НТВ

Introduction

The 144 million people of the Russian Federation have witnessed dramatic changes to their country's political, economic and legal systems in recent years. Since the dissolution of the Soviet Union in 1991, a new form of government elected by popular vote has emerged, the economy has been opened up to the free market, and a new Constitution and many legal reforms have been introduced.

For the people of this vast and diverse country, these changes have affected almost every aspect of their lives. Economic liberalization has brought new opportunities for some, while many face increased hardship and insecurity. In the political sphere there has been a marked increase in freedom of expression and movement. There has also been a growth in nationalist and separatist movements. On the human rights front, some of the gross violations for so long associated with the former Soviet Union have been eradicated, but widespread abuses by Russian law enforcement officials and security forces persist, often in a climate of impunity.

This report, which was written in late June 2002, focuses on specific and serious violations of international human rights and humanitarian law by Russian law enforcement and security forces. Throughout, it seeks to highlight the lack of accountability for the perpetrators. Investigating allegations of violations of human rights and humanitarian law independently, impartially, thoroughly, and promptly and holding those responsible for human rights violations to account, are key obligations under international law. The failure to fulfil these obligations is a major factor contributing to the persistence of such violations. The report also emphasizes the obstacles faced by victims, particularly women, children and members of ethnic minorities, in obtaining redress and the measures required to enable them to see justice done.

Demonstrators rally in support of NTV, a popular national independent television network, which was taken over by the state-controlled gas giant, Gazprom. The sign reads "Children of Russia for NTV". Journalists, fearing that their independent voice was under threat, joined the rally. April 2001.

1

© AFP

The first main section of the report (Chapter 2) focuses on the widespread torture and ill-treatment of women, men and children in custody. A wide range of coercive methods is used to extract confessions which are then used to secure convictions. Victims are frequently denied rights guaranteed under national and international law which serve, among other things, as safeguards against torture, such as prompt access to a lawyer. In practice the authorities do little to protect detainees.

A group of elderly women try to make ends meet by selling soft drinks to passers-by near Red Square, Moscow, March 2000. Economic reforms have had a negative effect on many people in Russia during the past decade.

The suffering continues in Russia's overcrowded and disease-ridden prisons, where almost a million people languish. Conditions are generally so appalling in pre-trial detention centres that they amount to cruel, inhuman and degrading treatment.

In the conflict in Chechnya, the focus of Chapter 3, the disregard for human rights and dignity long experienced in the Russian Federation has reached alarming levels. The conflict has been characterized by widespread human rights abuses by both sides. Credible reports speak of Russian security forces as responsible for attacks against civilians, rape and other forms of torture, "disappearances" and extrajudicial executions — all serious breaches of international humanitarian law. The perpetrators of such crimes have been able to act with virtual impunity. For reasons of political expediency, this dismal human rights record of Russia's security forces is being largely ignored by governments around the world.

Chechen forces are also reported to have committed human rights abuses, including hostage-taking, killing captured Russian soldiers and targeting civilian members of the Chechen administration.

This report ends with a series of recommendations to the Russian authorities that, if implemented, would help protect the human rights of everyone in Russia. It also includes recommendations to the Chechen forces. In addition, Amnesty International is calling on the international community to put pressure on the Russian Federation to live up to its obligations under international law to respect, protect, ensure and promote human rights.

Amnesty International's work

"Influenced by (my wife) Lusia, and my colleagues and friends, I have devoted more and more attention to individual victims of injustice. I support Amnesty International's call for the release of prisoners of conscience everywhere, as well as its efforts to end the death penalty and the use of torture. I am convinced that only an 'ideology of human rights' can unite people without regard to nationality, political convictions, religion, or social status."
Andrey Sakharov, former prisoner of conscience and leading human rights activist [1]

In compiling this report, Amnesty International has drawn on many years of work monitoring the human rights situation in the Russian Federation, including research into individual cases. Amnesty International cooperates with a number of human rights organizations working both within the Russian Federation and as part of the international human rights movement and is grateful for their assistance.

Amnesty International conducts its research on Russia through a combination of field research trips, contacts with human rights organizations and others based in Russia, checking information sent directly to Amnesty International's International Secretariat in London, and daily monitoring of news from the country. During research trips, Amnesty International delegates interview victims of human rights violations, their relatives and lawyers in order to gain first-hand information about the alleged violation. They also meet state officials to raise Amnesty International's concerns, obtain information and engage the authorities in finding a solution.

Since the second conflict began, the security situation in Chechnya and obstacles to access there imposed by the Russian authorities have constrained direct monitoring by international human rights organizations. As a result, Amnesty International has conducted research visits in the neighbouring Republic of Ingushetia where many Chechens have fled to avoid the fighting and abuses. Most of the testimony in the chapter on Chechnya was obtained in the camps for displaced Chechens in and around Nazran, Ingushetia. Other displaced Chechens were interviewed in private homes and unofficial settlements.

Amnesty International has published a wide variety of materials on Russia over the years. These have included regular updates on the human rights situation in the twice-yearly *Concerns in Europe* bulletin, along with numerous urgent appeals for people in danger of serious human rights violations such as torture or extrajudicial execution. Some documents have highlighted the cases of individuals, such as prisoner of conscience Aleksandr Nikitin.[2] Others have examined broader issues, such as torture and ill-treatment in the army, conscientious objection or the prevalence of torture and ill-treatment in the penitentiary system.[3] Other reports have documented the organization's concerns during the conflicts in Chechnya.[4]

The publication of this report coincides with the launch of a major worldwide campaign by Amnesty International on human rights in the Russian Federation. The campaign seeks to highlight the discrepancy between the human rights protection which those living in Russia have in international and national law, and the reality of widespread human rights abuses committed by agents of the state and private individuals or groups (non-state actors) in a climate of impunity. Amnesty International members around the world will be urging the government to live up to its obligations to protect, respect, ensure and promote human rights so that there is *justice for everybody*.

In December 2001 Amnesty International delegates took part in a three-day public event in Moscow, urging the Russian government to abolish the death penalty. The series of activities, launched on Human Rights Day, included the presentation of an open letter to the State *Duma* (parliament), participation in conferences organized by the Council of Europe and the State *Duma* Committee for Legislation, and a series of meetings with government officials, members of the judiciary, various religious leaders, students and the media. Three leading campaigners for the abolition of the death penalty from the USA also attended the event at the invitation of Amnesty International.

Chapter 1: Background

Inside Russia

The Russian Federation emerged as a sovereign state from the collapsing Soviet Union in 1991. A new Constitution adopted in 1993 made Russia a federal presidential republic with a bicameral legislature. The current President, Vladimir Putin, was elected by popular vote in March 2000 and is serving a four-year term.

Russia is by area the world's largest country, spanning 11 time zones and stretching from the Baltic Sea and St Petersburg in the northwest, to Vladivostok on the Pacific Ocean in the southeast. It is divided into 89 constituent parts — 49 *oblasts* (regions), 21 republics, 10 autonomous *okrugs* (districts), six *krais* (territories), two federal cities and one autonomous *oblast*.

The population of 144 million is extremely diverse in ethnic and religious terms, with people coming from around 100 distinct ethnic or national backgrounds. These include ethnic Russians (around 84 per cent of the population), Ukrainians, Tatars, Chuvashians, Bashkirians, Belarusians, Moldovans and Kalmykians.

The majority religion is Orthodox Christian, and the Russian Orthodox Church plays a prominent role in Russian society. An estimated 19 per cent of the population are Muslims, while smaller numbers are Jews, Buddhists and members of other religious groups.

Since 1991, Russia has undergone substantial political, economic, legal and cultural change. In the 1980s the General Secretary of the Communist Party, Mikhail Gorbachev, led attempts to reform the system of communism that had prevailed for decades. This was followed by the mass privatization of state industries and the consolidation of a market economy under President Boris Yeltsin.

These reforms have had a profound impact on the everyday lives of the general population. There were widespread accusations that the privatization process was corrupt and unfair. The state infrastructure, particularly in healthcare and education, was particularly badly hit, and many state employees were not paid for months. As the economy contracted on a massive scale, unemployment soared and there was a dramatic rise in the number of people thrown into poverty. The collapse of the ruble in August 1998, prompted by default on loan payments to international financial institutions, wiped out people's savings and shattered confidence in the government's economic management. However, the economy has since enjoyed a degree of stability.

Chechnya has been the subject of political, economic and military turmoil since the collapse of the Soviet Union. The first conflict broke out in 1994 when Russian forces were sent to the region to regain control of the republic following the then Chechen President's declaration of independence from the Russian Federation. The conflict lasted two years and cost thousands of lives. The Russian military crack-down failed to subdue Chechen forces and a compromise agreement was signed to end a conflict that was increasingly unpopular in Russia.

In September 1999 the Russian authorities again sent troops to Chechnya. This followed attacks, reportedly by up to 1,000 Chechen fighters, in neighbouring Dagestan, and a series of bombings of apartment blocks in Moscow and two other cities which were blamed by the Russian authorities on "Chechens". This second armed conflict in Chechnya shows no sign of abating. Some 300,000 people have been displaced during the conflict.

The international context

A major nuclear power and one of five permanent members of the UN Security Council, Russia retains an important place on the international stage. In the post-Soviet era, Russia has sought to reassert its position as a global player in trade and international relations. For example, it has joined the G8 grouping of wealthy, industrialized nations, and has contributed troops to international peacekeeping operations to countries following armed conflicts, such as those in Bosnia and Kosovo.

Russia is one of the world's top three producers of military, security and police (MSP) equipment. It is also a leading exporter of such equipment. For example, it is second only to

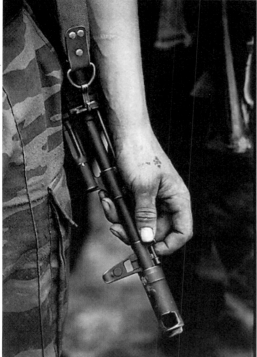

© Leo Erken/Panos Pictures

the USA as a supplier of light weapons and ammunition.[5] Russian MSP equipment is actively promoted, including at recent arms fairs in the Middle East, Asia, Africa and Latin America. The majority of the Russian Federation's military exports are made via the state-controlled organization *Rosoboronexport* which has agents in 36 countries.[6]

Evidence of Russian weapons exports being used for human rights violations has been widely documented.[7] The Russian government does not have a formal system of arms exports based on international human rights standards and international humanitarian law,

A soldier at an army base in Khankala, near Grozny in Chechnya, July 2000. Russia is one of the world's top three producers of military, security and police equipment.

but in 1993 it agreed to the terms of the Organization for Security and Co-operation in Europe (OSCE) Principles Governing Conventional Arms Transfers which call for arms exports to be prevented if they are likely to be used for human rights violations.[8] In November 2000 Russia agreed to submit to the OSCE appropriate data on all small arms and light weapons transfers. However, doubts continue as to whether deeds will match words.

International standards

The Soviet Union signed and ratified a number of international human rights treaties between the 1960s and 1991. However, for decades the authorities largely ignored the obligations they had undertaken and human rights at home saw little or no improvement. The break-up of the Soviet Union in 1991 brought renewed hopes that the political will to turn these human rights commitments into reality would emerge.

"Providing respect for the whole range of human rights and freedoms is not an internal matter for any one state, but it is their duty under the statute of the United Nations, the international covenants and conventions."
President Boris Yeltsin, addressing the UN Security Council in 1992 [9]

In a January 1992 communication to diplomatic missions in Moscow, the Russian government declared that it would continue to "perform the rights and to fulfil the obligations following from the international agreements signed by the USSR". These agreements included several key international human rights treaties:

- International Covenant on Civil and Political Rights
- International Covenant on Economic, Social and Cultural Rights
- International Convention on the Elimination of All Forms of Racial Discrimination
- Convention on the Elimination of All Forms of Discrimination against Women
- Convention against Torture and Other Cruel, Inhuman or Degrading Treatment or Punishment
- Convention on the Rights of the Child

The Soviet Union also ratified the 1949 Geneva Conventions and their two Additional Protocols. Following accession to the Council of Europe in 1996, Russia ratified the European Convention for the Protection of Human Rights and Fundamental Freedoms and a number of other Council of Europe treaties aimed at the protection of human rights.

Since the Russian Federation became a member of the Council of Europe, its human rights record, including law and policy and their implementation, have been subject to regular and increased scrutiny. There have been many important initiatives, but these have not brought an end to widespread human rights violations.

When it acceded to the Council of Europe on 28 February 1996 the Russian Federation officially committed itself to suspending all executions, pending the full abolition of the death penalty within three years; between 1962 and 1989, 24,422 people had reportedly been executed in the Soviet Union.[10] A moratorium was introduced and executions stopped in August 1996. However, the death penalty has not yet been abolished in law and the current moratorium on executions is a fragile guarantee against the renewed use of capital punishment.

Conscientious objection to military service is recognized as a legitimate exercise of the right to freedom of thought, conscience and religion guaranteed under Article 18 of the International Covenant on Civil and Political Rights to which Russia is a party. The right to alternative service on grounds of conscience or religious belief is also recognized in the Russian Constitution.[11] Although the Russian *Duma* (parliament) approved a bill in mid-2002 that permits alternative civilian service that is substantially longer than military service — three and a half years, as opposed to two years[12] — the bill's provisions were not expected to be implemented until late 2003.

"The term 'discrimination'... should be understood to imply any distinction, exclusion, restriction or preference which is based on any ground such as race, colour, sex, language, religion, political or other opinion, national or social origin, property, birth or other status, and which has the purpose of nullifying or impairing the recognition, enjoyment or exercise by all persons, on an equal footing, of all rights and freedoms."
General Comment 18, Human Rights Committee

Under international human rights law, governments are obliged to tackle discrimination in all its forms. Governments have a responsibility to ensure that laws and institutions of the state address the root causes of discrimination. Despite this, discrimination continues to manifest itself in Russia through violence in a variety of forms, including violence against women and racist assaults. Whether inflicted during armed conflict, in custody, in the community or in the home, this violence is intimately linked to the subordinate or marginalized position which those targeted for discrimination hold in society. As in other cases of human rights violations in Russia, the lack of accountability for those who abuse women, children and ethnic or other minorities has served to exacerbate the problem and help create a climate of impunity.

© AP

Discrimination on the basis of religious identity persists and many religious groups perceived as non-indigenous and in competition with the Orthodox Church, including the Salvation Army, Jehovah's Witnesses and, more recently, officials of the Roman Catholic Church, face harassment.

As a state party to the International Convention on the Elimination of All Forms of Racial Discrimination, the Russian government is obliged to take positive measures to prevent discrimination on grounds of "race, colour, descent, or national or ethnic origin" and to guarantee to everyone equality before the law.[13] However, Amnesty International continues to receive reports of discrimination and ethnically motivated violence by agents of the state and non-state actors in Moscow, St Petersburg and other cities across the Russian Federation. Victims whose cases have come to the attention of Amnesty International are predominantly students and refugees from Africa, but also include people from the north and south Caucasus (including ethnic Chechens), Central Asia, Asia, the Middle East and Central America. Although less frequently the subject of personal physical attacks, Jews have

A survivor of trafficking speaks to journalists in Moscow at the launch of a campaign by a coalition of women's groups to fight trafficking in women, May 2001. Every year a reported 50,000 women and girls from the 15 states which formerly made up the Soviet Union are sent into sexual slavery all over the world. The woman asked that her identity be withheld, fearing persecution by the traffickers.

© AI

The Meskhetians, a largely Muslim group, were deported from southwest Georgia in 1944. Many of those who settled in Uzbekistan were subsequently forced to flee to Russia in 1989. As citizens of the former Soviet Union who were permanently residing in the Russian Federation when the 1992 citizenship law was adopted, they are by law Russian citizens. However, the authorities in Krymsk Region of Krasnodar Territory have persistently denied local Meskhetians their legal rights and their rights to citizenship. In practice this means that people like Begzadi and Sultan Akhmedov (*pictured*) are denied access to pensions, state medical care and legal employment and cannot officially register house or land purchases, marriages or deaths.

been subjected to anti-Semitic verbal abuse and attacks on their religious buildings.

Many racist attacks are not reported to the police. This particularly applies to refugees, who have a justified fear that any approach to the police will lead to harassment and extortion because their identity papers are often not accepted as valid by the police. Refugees also know from experience that the police are reluctant to classify such attacks as racially motivated. Highly placed police officials have frequently and publicly described racist attackers as mere drunken "hooligans".

The Russian authorities are also failing in their obligation to protect women from violence in the home. Russia is a state party to the Convention on the Elimination of All Forms of Discrimination against Women and as such is obliged to submit reports every four years to the Committee on the Elimination of Discrimination against Women. In January 2002 the Committee expressed serious concern at Russia's failure to implement the provisions of the Convention, especially in the area of domestic violence against women — in their report submitted to the Committee, the Russian authorities stated that 14,000 women die each year at the hands of their husbands or other relatives.[14] In its concluding observations the Committee stated that it "is concerned at the prevalent tendency, including by law enforcement officials to view [domestic] violence not as a crime but as a private matter between spouses".[15] The Committee recommended, among other measures, that the Russian government immediately enact "specific domestic violence legislation to facilitate the prosecution of offenders" and take "immediate and effective measures to provide training to all levels of law enforcement officers and judges as to the serious and criminal nature of domestic violence".[16]

Russia has ratified the Convention on the Rights of the Child, yet children are not afforded many of the special rights guaranteed in the Convention to protect them from torture, ill-treatment and other violations of their human rights. In 1999 the Committee on the Rights of the Child expressed concern at allegations of the "widespread practice of torture and ill-treatment" against children.[17] The Committee also expressed concern about reports of extended periods of pre-trial detention of juveniles at the discretion of the procurator, and about poor conditions in places of detention and prisons.[18] The Committee was further concerned about allegations that the conditions in which children were held, particularly in detention facilities but also in institutions in general, amounted to inhuman or degrading treatment.[19] The Committee urged the Russian authorities to ensure that, in dispensing juvenile justice, children are only deprived of their liberty as a measure of last resort. It also emphasized the need to change the punitive character of juvenile justice to a system aimed more at the rehabilitation of juvenile offenders.[20]

It is clear, then, that there is a wide disparity between the international human rights obligations that Russia has promised to uphold, and the reality on the ground. The authorities need to send a clear message to their law enforcement and security forces that they must respect human rights in all circumstances, and that all those who do not will be made to answer for their actions in a court of law. In addition, the authorities must act with due diligence to protect, ensure and fulfil the rights of all people in its territories — including ethnic and national minorities; lesbian, gay, bisexual and transgender people; women; and children — in order to protect them from discrimination.

Chapter 2: Torture and ill-treatment in custody

"They brought out an apparatus, some kind of box with wires and plugged it into a socket. One of them held me, while the second attached the wires to my ears and turned on the power. After a little while they turned it off. They turned it on and off periodically and in the intervals asked me whether I would confess or not. They continually increased the length and force of the shocks. And when I could bear it no longer, I confessed to the murder and said that I would sign everything... Then they started to torture me further... At that moment, when I was almost unconscious... I jumped up and leapt out of the window."

Aleksei Mikheev [21]

Aleksei Mikheev has been seeking justice without success for nearly four years for his treatment at the hands of police and the permanent paralysis he suffered. A 23-year-old part time student who also worked for the traffic police, he was arrested on 10 September 1998 in the city of Nizhnii Novgorod on suspicion of raping and murdering a 17-year-old girl. Ten days later, reportedly after several sessions of prolonged electro-shock torture at Leninskii district police station, Aleksei Mikheev jumped through the third-floor window of the police station and fractured his spine. The lower part of his body is now paralysed. According to Aleksei Mikheev, the girl he was alleged to have murdered appeared unharmed later on the day he jumped from the window and the investigation was closed.

After filing a complaint about his treatment with the Nizhnii Novgorod procuracy, two criminal cases were opened. The first related to allegations of falsifying a police report brought against three officers at the Bogorodsk police station where Aleksei Mikheev was first held. This investigation has reportedly been opened and closed several times.[22] The case was reportedly first closed because of a "change in circumstances" — the officers concerned had been

Police use batons to break up a demonstration in Moscow, 28 May 2002. The protesters represented a variety of organizations and included environmentalists, anarchists and anti-capitalists.

dismissed. The latest appeal against the decision to close the investigation resulted in the reopening of the investigation on 29 October 2001. At the time of writing, this investigation was still pending.

The second criminal case was opened on 21 September 1998 by the Leninskii district procuracy against the police officers of that district for driving Aleksei Mikheev to attempt suicide. This investigation was closed two months later owing to "lack of evidence". A series of investigations followed that were closed and then ordered reopened by various procuracies in Nizhnii Novgorod and the region. In total, the investigation into these allegations has been opened and closed at least six times, according to information available to Amnesty International.[23]

Aleksei Mikheev

Despite these repeated investigations and much evidence supporting his allegations, no one has been prosecuted, charged or suspended from duty for the torture of Aleksei Mikheev. A civil suit for damages is pending before the Russian courts. A case alleging that Aleksei Mikheev's rights under the European Convention on Human Rights (ECHR) were violated has been submitted to the European Court of Human Rights in Strasbourg, France.

Compelling information gathered by Amnesty International over recent years from victims and other sources attests to the widespread use of torture and ill-treatment by law enforcement officials across the Russian Federation. Torture and ill-treatment are frequently used by police to elicit confessions or incriminating information from suspects. There are also persistent reports of torture and ill-treatment in pre-trial detention centres and prisons. Overcrowding and insanitary conditions in pre-trial detention facilities (also known by the Russian acronym "SIZO"[24]) are generally so extreme that they amount to cruel, inhuman or degrading treatment or punishment. Poor conditions also prevail in prisons where infectious diseases are rife and medical treatment is inadequate.[25]

Torture is prohibited under Russian law. The clearest prohibition is set out in the 1993 Constitution. Article 21(2) states: "[N]o one shall be subjected to torture, violence or other cruel or degrading treatment or punishment. No one may be subjected to medical, scientific or other experiments without voluntary consent." However, the Criminal Code does not criminalize certain acts of torture and ill-treatment set out in Article 1 of the UN Convention against Torture. Article 117 of the Criminal Code, which refers to subjecting an individual to physical or psychological suffering through physical violence, comes closest to the definition in the Convention against Torture. Significantly, however, Article 117 does not criminalize the infliction of physical or psychological suffering by non-violent means.

The Russian Federation has ratified numerous international treaties that prohibit torture in all circumstances, including the Convention against Torture. Article 15(4) of the Russian Constitution states that international law takes precedence over domestic law and should be applied directly by the courts. However, in cases of torture the courts in Russia rely on the Criminal Code rather than international standards. In February 2002 the *Duma* voted against amending the Criminal Code to include a specific crime of torture.[26]

These gaps in Russian criminal law, in a country in which torture and ill-treatment are widespread, is clearly of great concern. At the time of writing (late June 2002), the criminal justice system was about to undergo radical changes with the introduction of a new Criminal Procedure Code (CPC — see box pp. 20 and 21). If implemented in full, Amnesty International is hopeful that some of the changes will address some of the shortfalls in the legal system that leave detainees at risk of torture and ill-treatment. However, the organization believes there are many factors that lie behind the prevalence of torture and ill-treatment, not least of these being the climate of impunity enjoyed by the perpetrators.

The new Criminal Procedure Code

In December 2001 the *Duma* approved the new CPC, ending years of debate. The new code, which replaces the CPC that came into force on 1 January 1961, introduces sweeping changes to the criminal justice system, such as mandating the introduction of jury trials for serious crimes throughout the country as of 1 January 2003. All the other new provisions are to be introduced on 1 July 2002.

Although there are concerns that the new code does not fully address all the shortfalls of the old CPC, it does contain important reforms, some of which are highlighted below.

- ## Courts to determine pre-trial detention

    Under the new CPC the courts, rather than the procuracy, will have responsibility for determining whether or not a suspect will be held in detention during an investigation. Previously, the procuracy was responsible for determining whether a person would be detained pending investigation as well as for investigating the case.

- ## A detainee must be brought before the court in person within 48 hours

    This is an important reform, since most torture and ill-treatment in custody happen in the first hours that a person is deprived of their liberty. Reducing the time a person is held without judicial review may help to reduce the incidence of torture and ill-treatment. Under the new CRC, suspects will appear in person in court in order for the court to determine whether or not they should be released and under what guarantees against flight, or whether they should be detained until trial. This appearance before a court will give victims of torture and ill-treatment a chance to inform the court about their treatment at a much earlier stage of the criminal justice process than before.

- ## The procurator has to be in court to prosecute

  Under the old CPC, in cases where the prosecutor (procurator) failed to appear in court, the judge was obliged to carry out the prosecutor's function as well as to issue the verdict. This system raised serious questions about independence and impartiality, especially in cases where the accused alleged that they had been tortured and ill-treated to force them to confess. If the judge accepted allegations of torture and ill-treatment by the defendant, the judge would be undermining the prosecution case which he or she was presenting.

- ## Court-appointed lawyer for the accused

  This is an important move to address allegations of collusion between the lawyers appointed by the police and the prosecution.

- ## Reversal of the burden of proof

  If a person alleges that a "confession" was extracted as a result of torture, the burden of proof for the allegations of torture is reversed under the new code. In other words, instead of the accused having to prove that their confession was not given freely, it will now be up to the law enforcement agencies to prove that the confession was not the result of torture or ill-treatment.

- ## Suspension of the trial

  If an accused person alleges during trial that he or she was tortured or ill-treated by law enforcement or investigative officers, under the new CPC the hearing will now have to be suspended while those allegations are investigated.

- ## Admissibility of evidence

  Any evidence obtained by an official during the investigative process in ways that violate the CPC, such as denying a suspect access to a lawyer or using torture or ill-treatment during questioning, will be inadmissible in court under the new code.

Methods of torture and ill-treatment

"When I refused [to write the confession], they handcuffed my hands behind my back and made me lie face down on the floor; they cuffed my legs... he put a gas mask on my face and turned off the air supply. The other policemen held me so I couldn't move. I lost consciousness... They did 'slonik'[27] on me five times; each time I lost consciousness I thought I was going to die. After lunch, they started to beat me again in a way so as not to leave any marks. They then did 'slonik' again another three times after which I lost consciousness. In the end, I couldn't hold out and agreed to write what they told me."
Aleksandr Shcherbakov, aged 25, describing how police officers forced him to write a "confession" to a series of burglaries[28]

The use of torture and ill-treatment in police custody to elicit "confessions" or incriminating information from suspects appears to be virtually routine. Beatings with fists and batons, along with kicking, are the most common forms of torture and ill-treatment reported to Amnesty International. However, police reportedly often use other torture methods to force suspects to confess, particularly methods that leave no physical traces or leave marks that will have disappeared by the time the victim has access to the outside world or is brought to court.

Victims have described to Amnesty International how they were partially asphyxiated in police custody to extract "confessions". One such method, known as "*slonik*" ("the elephant"), involves restraining the victim, forcibly placing a gas mask over the victim's head, and cutting off the air supply until they lose consciousness. The air supply is then restored. The torturers then threaten to turn it off again unless the victim signs a "confession". Variations of this technique include spraying tear-gas into the mask, which makes the victim vomit, or using a plastic bag instead of a gas mask.

"I was tortured with boiling water. They forced me to lie down on my back on the floor, with my hands behind my head, my legs held upwards vertically at 90 degrees to the floor. As soon as I was unable to hold this position and couldn't keep my legs vertical and bent them at the knees, they poured boiling water from a kettle on my stomach, demanding that I raise my legs and sign a blank form".[29]

Aleksei Golubkov, aged 33, was arrested by police in Moscow on 5 August 1997 and taken to Zhulebino police station. He alleges that during interrogation there, investigators and police officers tortured him to force him to "confess" to sexual crimes against minors.

He says he was beaten and kicked on his head and back until he lost consciousness. He was forced to lie in a contorted position on the floor and when he tried to move, investigators poured boiling water on his stomach. He was also forced to stand against a wall on one leg, with both arms outstretched; in punishment for not maintaining this position, boiling water was poured down his neck. He alleges that he then had a cellophane bag put over his head until he lost consciousness. While this was being done he was repeatedly asked to sign a statement.

Four days after the alleged torture, Aleksei Golubkov was taken to Medical Centre No.178 in Moscow, where doctors recommended immediate hospitalization for the injuries he had sustained. Reportedly as a result of police pressure, Aleksei Golubkov's burns and contusions were not recorded and he was not admitted to hospital for a further 48 hours. However, the injuries were subsequently recorded at Hospital No. 20 and at the medical ward of the pre-trial detention centre known as Matrosskaia Tishina where he was treated for around six weeks. At Hospital No. 20 he was diagnosed with second-degree multiple burns to the stomach and back, multiple fractures of the ribs, and bruising around the kidneys and liver.

On 19 May 1997 Aleksei Golubkov was sentenced to nine years' imprisonment for violent actions of a sexual character, linked with a threat of murder or causing serious physical harm committed against a minor under 14 years of age.[30]

Aleksei Golubkov, who protests his innocence, submitted a complaint about the torture he says he suffered to the Kuzminski District Procurator in Moscow, which in October 1997 opened a criminal investigation into the allegations of torture and ill-treatment. According to reports, the case (No. 157304) was subsequently closed on 1 October 1998 because of lack of evidence. On 24 June 2002 Aleksei Golubkov's mother told Amnesty International that he had refused the opportunity to be considered for parole as this requires an admission of guilt.

Another reported torture method is known as "*lastochka*" ("the swallow"). The detainee's arms are handcuffed behind the back in a raised position, and the person is then suspended by the arms from the wall or ceiling causing great pain. In some cases, the person is beaten while suspended. In the method known as "*konvert*" ("the envelope"), the person is forced to place their head between their knees, and their hands are handcuffed or tied to their ankles. They are then beaten in this position.

Other torture techniques reported to Amnesty International include sexual violence and rape, the use of electric shocks, striking on the head with hardback books, burning with cigarettes, beating with plastic bottles partially filled with water, and threats against the victim or their loved ones.

Amnesty International also continues to receive reports of incidents of torture and ill-treatment in SIZOs and in prisons, including cases related to special riot police deployed in prisons.

In June 2001 the Perm Regional Human Rights Centre reportedly received around 160 complaints from prisoners in the hard labour colony near the village of Tsepets, Perm region. The complaints related to prolonged beatings allegedly carried out between 17 and 19 April 2001 by eight masked members of a local prison unit of OMON (special riot police), known as "*Variag*". According to the inmates, nine prisoners required hospital treatment for injuries that included broken ribs and concussion.

A criminal investigation into the allegations began on 9 June 2001 under Article 286(3) of the Criminal Code which penalizes "exceeding authority with the use or threat of force". However, the investigation was subsequently closed on the grounds that none of the inmates could identify their masked attackers. Following the intervention of the Perm Human Rights Centre and the broadcasting of a news item on the case on national television, a senior official from the General Procuracy visited the colony. He reportedly ordered the reopening of the criminal investigation, which led to the head of the "*Variag*" unit being charged with the lesser crime of "negligence". He was tried and acquitted on 22 February 2002. At the time of writing, the results of challenges to the verdict, both from the inmates and the procurator, were pending.

Inmates of Women's Prison No. 15 in Samara return to the prison from the sewing factory where they work, February 2002.

Conditions of detention

Nearly a million men, women and children are incarcerated in Russia, including more than 200,000 awaiting trial.[31] Most of those in pre-trial detention are held in conditions that amount to cruel, inhuman or degrading treatment or punishment.[32]

A primary cause of such conditions is chronic overcrowding. Under the old CPC, which was operational until the end of June 2002, detention of suspects before trial has been the norm. The criminal justice system has been unable to cope with the investigation and trial of the large number of criminal cases within a reasonable time. This has inevitably led to prolonged periods of pre-trial detention.

In some cases, the appalling conditions in pre-trial detention contribute to detainees "confessing" in order to reduce the time they spend in SIZOs. For example, in the aftermath of the bombing of apartment blocks in Moscow in 1999, many Chechens admitted to crimes they had not committed (such as possession of bullets or small amounts of drugs) knowing they would receive a suspended sentence and thus be released. A typical response to suggestions that they should appeal against the conviction to clear their name was: "I appreciate your help, but I am just glad to be out. You didn't have to sit in that SIZO."

Describing conditions in pre-trial detention in his report of a visit to the Russian Federation in 1994, the UN Special Rapporteur on torture said:

"The conditions are cruel, inhuman and degrading; they are torturous. To the extent that suspects are confined there to facilitate the investigation by breaking their wills with a view to eliciting confessions and information, they can properly be described as being subjected to torture."[33]

Despite a series of amnesties since 1994 which have reduced the pre-trial detention population by around 60,000, the problem of overcrowding remains acute.[34]

A report by the Procurator-General, Vladimir Ustinov, submitted to the Federal Assembly in April 2002, admitted that prison conditions were not improving.[35] It also stated, "The average number of those in detention centres exceeds the legally prescribed norms by 50 per cent, and in Tatarstan and in Irkutsk, Nizhnii Novgorod, Tver and Chita Regions, Krasnodar Territory, Moscow and St Petersburg they are overcrowded by almost 250 per cent."

In many SIZOs chronic overcrowding forces detainees to sleep in shifts, as there are fewer beds than inmates, and encourages the spread of infectious diseases. In his April 2001 annual report, the human rights Ombudsman, Oleg Mironov, described pre-trial detention facilities as "hotbeds of epidemics". In April 2002 the UN Committee against Torture expressed concern about "distressing conditions" in pre-trial detention. In May 2002 the Deputy Justice Minister reported that over half of all prisoners in Russia were ill, including over 300,000 with mental illnesses, 92,000 with tuberculosis, 33,600 who were registered with HIV/AIDS, and 30,000 with syphilis.[36]

Some 20,000 women and girls are held in pre-trial detention facilities, where they are segregated from male detainees. According to a report by Penal Reform International (PRI) published in 1999, overcrowding in mixed facilities in Moscow and St Petersburg was particularly acute and was estimated at three times overcapacity. The report said that other mixed pre-trial detention facilities and two newer women-only facilities in Moscow and St Petersburg held 50 per cent more inmates than they were designed to house.[37]

Women and girls in prison colonies face additional problems. According to PRI, in 2001 approximately 40,000 women and girl prisoners were held in 35 remote prison colonies for women. There are only three prison colonies for convicted girls in the whole country, which means that girls as young as 13 are held hundreds or thousands of kilometres from their homes. This makes maintaining links with families or receiving material support difficult. In all these colonies, inmates suffer from inadequate nutrition, as well as poor hygiene and healthcare. Menstruating women are reportedly not provided with sanitary supplies and so resort to using rags or the stuffing of their mattresses. The European Committee for the Prevention of Torture and Inhuman or Degrading Treatment or Punishment (CPT) has stated that the failure to provide sanitary towels to female detainees amounted to degrading treatment.[38]

At risk of torture

Although anyone who comes into contact with law enforcement officials as a suspect or even a witness to a crime may be at risk of torture and ill-treatment, members of ethnic minorities and the poor are particularly at risk. The special safeguards outlined in international human rights standards to protect women and children from abuse in custody should apply in Russia, according to the 1993 Constitution, but are not respected in practice.

Women

> "*They beat me because I tried to resist and tried to see who they were... They beat me about the head, on the neck from behind so I wouldn't move my head. They punched me and hit me in the ribs constantly. One would rape me while the other held me down, pushing my face into the bed.*"
>
> Marina T. [39]

Women in police custody have been subjected to torture, including rape and other sexual violence. Such abuses are facilitated by the frequent failure of the authorities to ensure that women deprived of their liberty are informed of their right to a lawyer; that they are interrogated in the presence of their lawyer; and that they are attended by women staff.[40] The abuses are also made more likely by the lack of gender-specific information in programs to educate and train officials regarding the prohibition of torture and ill-treatment.

The risks facing female detainees are compounded by the notorious reluctance of procurators to investigate thoroughly allegations by women that they have suffered sexual and other abuses in police custody. In 2002 the Committee on the Elimination of Discrimination against Women (CEDAW) expressed concern "about the reports of ill-treatment of women in pre-detention centres and in prisons". The Committee also stated it was "deeply concerned by the fact that, despite credible evidence that police officials have used violence against women in custody, the Government has not, as a rule, investigated, disciplined or prosecuted offenders."[41]

On the night of 5 March 1999 in the city of Yaroslavl', traffic police stopped 20-year-old Marina T. in a friend's car, apparently suspecting that she was drunk, and took her to a sobering-up facility run by the Interior Ministry.[42] Once there, she says, three officers and a medical practitioner forcibly stripped her naked. They hit her head against the wall and punched her in the face. The officers who had originally detained her then tied her hands behind her back and dragged her by the hair into an adjoining room and threw her, face down, on to a small bed. There, Marina T. says she was raped by four men; among her attackers were the officers who had stopped the car.

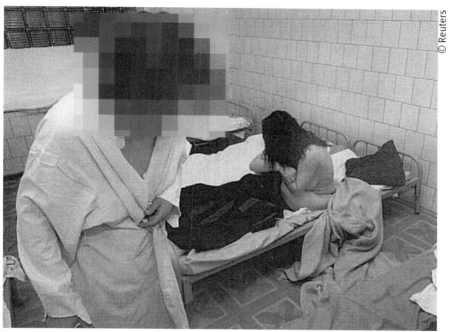

Inside an official sobering-up centre in Moscow, 1998.

Marina T. says that the men then in turn forced their penises into her mouth while grabbing her by the ears. She says that at this point she lost consciousness and when she came around, she was alone in the room. After she shouted to be released, the police officers returned and tied her more tightly to the bed. When this did not stop her screams, one of the men put a towel soaked in alcohol on to her face in an apparent attempt to subdue her.

Marina T. appeared before the Zavolzhskii district court the following morning accused of being drunk in a public place and of violent conduct towards the officers. The court fined her 800 rubles (around US$25) and ordered her to pay 50 rubles for the cost of staying at the sobering-up facility. She was then released. Marina T. says that during the court hearing she attempted to describe her torture to the judge, but that he interrupted her and accused her of being abusive towards the police officers before they detained her.

However, later that day Marina T. went to the local procuracy to file a complaint. The bruising to her face was noted. A criminal case was opened on 9 March 1999 against three police officers for torture and ill-treatment, but these charges were dropped on 18 May 2000 for lack of evidence. The officers reportedly remained under investigation, however, on charges of abuse of office and premeditated infliction of bodily harm — charges that carry lighter sentences than ill-treatment or rape.

Marina T. told Amnesty International that during the investigation, the police officers destroyed evidence, gave false statements to the procuracy, and threatened and intimidated Marina T. and others who were present in the sobering-up station that night.

The case was sent back and forth for investigation several times before the final hearing in March 2002 — some two years after Marina T. had lodged her complaint — at the Zavolzhskii district court. The court found one officer guilty of premeditated infliction of bodily harm — but released him immediately under an amnesty covering non-serious offences. Two other officers were found guilty of abuse of office with the use of violence and threats of violence — and were given suspended sentences and stripped of the right to work as police officers for two years.

The procuracy and Marina T.'s lawyer both challenged the verdicts. On 16 April 2002 the Yaroslavl' regional court annulled the verdicts and sent the case back to the Zavolzhskii court for retrial by different judges. As of mid-2002, the retrial of the three officers was still pending. Two other officers whom Marina T. says were among the four men who raped her have never been charged at all.

Children

"When you go to the procuracy, say to them that you took your child home, that he fell there and broke his vertebrae".

The words of a police-appointed lawyer reportedly advising the mother of 16-year-old Sergei Kalinin to keep quiet about the treatment of her son in police custody[43]

Under international standards that the Russian Federation has ratified, children are entitled to special protection, including against torture and ill-treatment, because their youth makes them particularly vulnerable to abuse. Yet children who are picked up by Russian police are denied this special protection. For example, in cases known to Amnesty International children have been denied one of the most basic protections — having a lawyer and an adult relative or appropriate adult present during questioning — which among other things serves as a safeguard

© AI

Young detainees in a pre-trial detention centre, 1999. Most children detained awaiting trial in Russia are kept in appalling conditions.

against torture and ill-treatment. Amnesty International has documented cases where children have been tortured or ill-treated by police in such circumstances.

Amnesty International's concerns about the abuse of children's rights in police custody were reflected by the Concluding Observations of the UN Committee on the Rights of the Child in 1999 on Russia's implementation of the Convention on the Rights of the Child. The Committee expressed concern at "allegations of the widespread practice of torture and ill-treatment" against children.[44]

Such findings are particularly disturbing given the scale of arrests and detention of children in Russia. More than a million juveniles[45] were reportedly charged by the police in 2001.[46]

On 14 September 2000 Sergei Kalinin, aged 16, together with three friends, allegedly stole a car in the Fili-Davidkovo district of Moscow. Police officers stopped the car and detained Sergei Kalinin and a 20-year-old man. Sergei Kalinin was detained for 24 hours in the Fili-Davidkovo police station, during which time the police did not inform the procurator.[47] During this period, Sergei Kalinin alleges that police officers beat him on his back and head, apparently to force him to confess to stealing a number of other cars. The officers also reportedly banged his head against a wall several times. Released the following day, Sergei Kalinin was taken to a treatment centre by his mother where he was diagnosed as having compressed fractures of the vertebrae.

On 16 September 2000 Sergei Kalinin was called in for questioning by a central investigative officer of the Interior Ministry. He was reportedly asked why his testimony differed to that given on 14 September. Sergei Kalinin's lawyer reportedly replied that the original testimony was obtained under duress involving beatings.

On 28 May 2001 the Kuntsevskii municipal court found Sergei Kalinin guilty of theft under Article 158(3) of the Criminal Code and sentenced him to three years' imprisonment in a prison colony for juveniles. After an appeal on 17 July 2001, Sergei Kalinin was released on a suspended sentence.

During the court hearing, and in meetings with the procuracy, Sergei Kalinin complained about the torture he suffered at the police station. However, at the time of writing there has been no criminal investigation into his allegations. According to his mother, Sergei Kalinin is still in pain as a result of the torture he suffered.

Tens of thousands of children are deprived of their liberty in Russia, despite the fact that Russia is obliged, under Article 37(b) of the Convention on the Rights of the Child, to ensure that, "[t]he arrest, detention or imprisonment of a child... shall be used only as a measure of last resort and for the shortest appropriate period of time." Children in Russia are routinely deprived of their liberty for months or even years in pre-trial detention and sentenced to long terms of imprisonment for relatively minor offences. In mid-2001 there were more than 17,000 children serving prison sentences in 64 special colonies for juveniles, according to the Justice Ministry. Many more were held in SIZOs. Like adults, most are crammed into overcrowded, dirty, badly ventilated and vermin-infested cells — conditions that are cruel, inhuman and degrading.[48] However, there have been some improvements in the way young prisoners are treated. For example, reports indicate that children are no longer held in solitary confinement or disciplinary isolation cells as punishment.

Once in SIZOs or prisons, children are vulnerable to abuse by both warders and other inmates. For example, 14-year-old Olga Mazalova was covered in bruises when she spoke to an Amnesty International delegate visiting Tomsk prison colony for girls in July 1999. She said she had been beaten in a punishment cell a few days earlier.

Ethnic minorities

"These Tajik drug dealers should all be shot."
The words of a doctor examining Azizkhon Davlatov and Samad and Iskandar Ibroimov, who were taken to hospital after reportedly being beaten by law enforcement officials in July 2000

People belonging to certain ethnic groups or nationalities, including Chechens and other Russian citizens, as well as migrant workers from territories of the former Soviet Union and refugees from further afield, have been stereotyped by Russian law enforcement officials as "terrorists", drug dealers or other types of criminal. The result has been the use of "racial profiling" — the widespread targeting by police of people, often on the basis of physical appearance, for checks of their homes and personal documents in relation to "registration". Those targeted by police are then at risk of human rights abuses such as arbitrary arrest, torture and ill-treatment.

There is a consensus of concern that discriminatory practices are linked with the registration system and its enforcement, particularly in Moscow. In 1991 the *"propiska"* system, under which people had to register their place of residence and were not allowed to move or change it without official permission, was abolished. However, variants of this system are still being enforced by some local governments.[49]

The European Commission against Racism and Intolerance expressed concern in 2001 that members of "visible minorities", particularly in big cities and some southern regions, appeared to be "disproportionately affected by the way the police (militia) enforce the system of registration of residence and temporary stay". It added that "the police can stop people and check their personal documents, search their homes, detain them and impose sanctions, which are reported to be often arbitrary and to result in request for bribes and extortion of money". It also noted that in this context members of "visible minorities" appeared to be disproportionately subject to arbitrary arrest and detention, and that there had been reports of torture and ill-treatment by police of those detained.[50]

On 4 July 2000 a group of unidentified men entered a house in Starbeevo village, Khimki district where Tajik construction workers lived, and reportedly insulted and severely beat three men — Azizkhon Davlatov and Samad and Iskandar Ibroimov — before taking them away. The group also reportedly smashed furniture and removed personal belongings. It subsequently emerged that the men

Adefers Dessu and his wife, Sarah, shown at a soup kitchen in Moscow where they work as volunteers helping to provide hot food to the city's elderly and homeless people. In the photograph Adefers Dessu is showing the injuries he suffered in February 2001, when he and his wife were attacked and beaten by a gang of youths armed with chains. Like many victims of racist attacks in Russia, the couple faced reluctance by both police and medical staff to register the incident as racially motivated. Sarah and Adefers Dessu came to Russia to escape political persecution in their native Ethiopia and Eritrea.

© Paula Allen

© AI

Bektash Fasylov was among five Meskhetians from Krymsk Region of Krasnodar Territory who were hospitalized with concussion after an unprovoked attack by a group of at least 60 self-styled cossacks in November 2001. There have been many reports that members of such groups often accompany police on local operations, dressing in military-style camouflage dress and black berets. Official complaints about the incident were lodged with the police. However, by mid-2002 no one had been brought to justice for the attack.

in the group were police officers led by a major from the 4th division of Moscow Region's organized crime squad (RUBOP).[51]

Azizkhon Davlatov and Samad and Iskandar Ibroimov were taken by the RUBOP officers to the Khimki Department of Internal Affairs, where the staff reportedly refused to admit them because of their visible injuries. The three men were taken to hospital in Khimki town, where the doctor pronounced them fit to be detained. They were subsequently charged with drugs offences.

On 14 July a lawyer, Inna Ailamazian, was engaged on the men's behalf by the Russian human rights organization Memorial. She says that the authorities did not permit her to see the men until 4 August. When she did see them that day, Samad Ibroimov complained of loss of sight in his right eye, constant headaches and pain in his left side. He told her that on 4 and 5 July he had been kicked and beaten about the head with a plastic bottle filled with water. She said that Iskandar Ibroimov had abrasions on his legs and Azizkhon Davlatov could hardly move and had marks of cigarette burns. The men had reportedly received no medical attention, despite demands by Inna Ailamazian from 14 July that they be medically examined.

© AP

The three men said that after they had been detained, the RUBOP officers asked for money "to buy them out" and that when it became clear that the men did not have the money, the officers then tortured and ill-treated them to make them confess to possessing, using and selling drugs.

Masked and armed police officers during a raid on the offices of the parent company of NTV, a television station known for its criticism of the government.

After two months in detention the men were released. On 29 September 2000 it was announced that, after an investigation by the Moscow district procuracy, the case against the three men had been closed for lack of evidence. At the same time it was announced that the actions of the RUBOP officers who carried out the 4 July operation would be investigated.

After the matter was taken out of the hands of the district and regional branches of the procuracy and transferred to the procuracy of the Central Region of the Russian Federation, a case was finally opened against three RUBOP officers in relation to fabrication of evidence, exceeding authority, theft and extortion.

On 11 March 2002 the trial of the three accused officers began in Khimki court. The lawyer for the victims applied for the accused RUBOP officers to be detained. She told the court that Azizkhon Davlatov, Samad and Iskandar Ibroimov, and the main witness, Abduzair Gaibnazarov (also a Tajik), had been harassed and detained by police before an earlier hearing, preventing their appearance at that hearing. She also described how Abduzair Gaibnazarov had been knocked unconscious in another incident involving a policeman and two men in civilian clothes. However, the application to have the RUBOP officers detained was turned down. As of June 2002 the case was pending but the officers were believed to have been detained.[52]

Why torture happens

Suspects are most at risk of torture and ill-treatment in the hours immediately following arrest, when they are being questioned and before formal charges have been filed. At the time of writing it was unclear to what degree the new CPC, which shortens this period, will stop this practice. Some of the factors that Amnesty International considers contribute to patterns of torture and ill-treatment are summarized below.

- **Pressure to convict**

  There is a rising fear in society at large about crime levels and poorly paid and inadequately trained and resourced police are under intense pressure to solve crimes. Police are also, according to reports, promoted on the basis of the number of cases they "solve". Such factors appear to encourage the use of illegal methods, such as torture and ill-treatment, in order to elicit "confessions" quickly from suspects. The system of promotion may also have the effect of discouraging police from recording crimes they believe they cannot solve.

- **Acceptance of confessions extracted under torture**

  Article 302 of the Criminal Code specifically prohibits coercion, including the use of threats, humiliation or torture, to extract a confession. Article 50(2) of the Constitution and Article 20(3) of the old CPC also forbid eliciting statements by the use of force or threats. The new CPC makes this prohibition even more explicit. Article 15 of the Convention against Torture states: "Each State Party shall ensure that any statement which is established to have been made as a result of torture shall not be invoked as evidence in any proceedings, except against a person accused of torture as evidence that the statement was made."

Despite such clear laws, investigative police in Russia routinely use torture and ill-treatment to extract "confessions". Such methods are in effect tolerated by the courts, which accept "confessions" taken under duress as valid evidence, even if they are retracted in court by the defendant, and rarely take action in response to allegations of torture. There are widespread allegations of collusion between the procuracy and the police to secure convictions through illegal means, and to cover up complaints of torture and ill-treatment.

• Denial of access to lawyers

Article 48 of the Constitution guarantees detainees the right to a lawyer from the moment of detention. It states, "Every person who has been detained, taken into custody or charged with a crime shall have the right to legal counsel from the moment of, respectively, detention or indictment". However, many suspects in police custody have complained that they were either not provided with a lawyer or were given a lawyer who was clearly working in collusion with the police. In other cases, detainees have said that they did not ask for legal representation out of fear that such a request would result in further torture and ill-treatment by the police. Some lawyers have told Amnesty International that they believe they have been deliberately obstructed from making contact with their clients, for example by being kept waiting for long periods on spurious grounds when they tried to visit their clients.

The right to a lawyer is not, however, afforded to those called in for questioning as witnesses. Anyone asked to come to a police station as a witness is obliged to do so, and what may appear to be an innocuous request can have very serious consequences. According to reports, the witness often becomes a suspect, yet their status as a witness means that they have no right to a lawyer during questioning. There is also no express requirement in Russian law for a lawyer to be present during the writing and signing of confessions.

- **Denial of access to medical professionals**
  Detainees are often not asked whether they wish to be examined by a medical professional before, during or after questioning. Prompt medical examination of people deprived of their liberty can be an effective safeguard against torture and ill-treatment, as underlined in international instruments such as the UN Body of Principles for the Treatment of All Persons under Any Form of Detention or Imprisonment.[53]

- **Suspects not informed of their rights**
  Under Article 51 of the Constitution, police are obliged to inform detainees of their rights, such as the right not to testify against oneself or close relatives. However, in practice suspects are usually not informed of their rights, including their right to bring a complaint against the authorities for torture and ill-treatment. Article 11(1) of the new CPC requires the court, procurator and investigator to inform a suspect of their rights.[54]

- **Prolonged pre-trial detention**
  Under the old CPC the procuracy, rather than the court, decided within 48 hours of arrest on the "means of restraint".[55] In law, the procuracy could choose between ordering a person to be detained or released on a written pledge not to flee. However, in practice, there was no presumption of liberty[56] — suspects were usually detained. Courts generally upheld the procurator's decision.

  The measures in place to guard against prolonged periods of pre-trial detention do not work. Under the old CPC the "means of restraint" should be reviewed by the procuracy every six months, but in reality the order to keep a suspect detained before trial has almost always been renewed. A bill approved by the *Duma* in February 2001 reduced the maximum length of pre-trial detention to one year, except for serious crimes where the limit was set at 18 months. However, the bill was not adopted after the Upper House failed to approve it. Under the new CPC the use of pre-trial detention is not permitted for offences carrying sentences of up to two years' imprisonment, except when there is a risk that the accused might not appear in court. The new code states that pre-trial detention should last a maximum of two months, although it may be extended to six months if the case is deemed to be complex. However, the Procurator-General can submit a request to a court to extend the period to 18 months.

Under the old CPC, a judge could order the case to be sent back to the procuracy for further investigation without ordering the release of the suspect, if the court decided that there was not enough evidence to convict.[57] Amnesty International has monitored cases during which this happened repeatedly and where delays in trial proceedings led to pre-trial detention periods of several years. As stated above, conditions in pre-trial detention in many facilities are such that they constitute cruel, inhuman or degrading treatment or punishment. The prospect of remaining in such conditions for prolonged periods has in effect coerced detainees into "confessing" to reduce the time spent in pre-trial detention.

No justice for the victims

"During the detention, the suspect tried to hide, and, in accordance with the Law on the Police, physical force was used, as a result of which Airapetian fell and broke his jaw".
Letter from the General Procuracy rebutting the allegations of torture and ill-treatment made by Tigran Airapetian[58]

Eighteen-year-old Tigran Airapetian was detained by a police officer at 11am on 10 February 2001 in his school yard in northern Moscow. He was accused of demanding money from an acquaintance, Evgennii Polukhin, in a dispute over a mobile telephone. The officer took Tigran Airapetian to Police Station No. 184, where he was reportedly beaten. Tigran Airapetian described how one officer then made him crouch down, forced him to extend his arms and placed a heavy door from a safe on them. When Tigran Airapetian could no longer support the weight of the door as instructed, the man reportedly kicked him in the chest and the others beat him.

Tigran Airapetian said that after this beating, and in a semi-conscious state, he signed a "confession" stating that he had extorted 500 rubles from Evgennii Polukhin with a threat of violence.[59] At approximately 10pm that evening a doctor reportedly told officers, "He'll live" after glancing at Tigran Airapetian from the cell door. However, another police officer took Tigran Airapetian to the local trauma unit where a doctor diagnosed that he had a broken jaw and recommended that an ambulance be called. However, the police officer took Tigran Airapetian back to the police station and again put him in a cell.

Soon after, at around 2am on 11 February, Tigran Airapetian was released. His father took him immediately to hospital where he underwent an operation and remained for over three weeks.

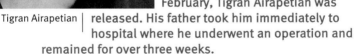

Tigran Airapetian

Tigran Airapetian filed a complaint on 21 May 2001 and the Butyrskii procuracy opened a criminal investigation into the allegations. However, despite Tigran Airapetian giving detailed descriptions and the names of the three men he identified as responsible, together with the address of the police station, on 23 August 2001 the Butyrskii procurator closed the preliminary investigation "until the persons accused of the offence are identified".

On 19 September 2001 Tigran Airapetian filed a complaint with the European Court of Human Rights in Strasbourg, France, claiming that his rights under the ECHR had been violated. At the time of writing, the case there was still pending.

Torture and ill-treatment persist so widely in Russia because the perpetrators almost always get away with their crimes. Preliminary inquiries into allegations of torture are in general superficial, often resulting in no formal or criminal investigation. Even when criminal investigations are held, the cases are frequently closed owing to "lack of evidence". Victims who continue to seek justice find themselves spending years going through seemingly endless rounds of investigations, rejections and appeals, and the rare convictions of torturers usually result in light sentences that are not commensurate with the gravity of the crime. This creates a climate of impunity for torturers, who have little or no fear that they will be held to account for their actions.

There are many factors that contribute to the climate of impunity for torturers, some of which are summarized below.

- ## Victims do not lodge complaints

  Some victims do not lodge complaints either because they do not know they can, or because they fear retribution if they do. Others have no confidence that any complaint they might make will result in justice being done, so they do not make the effort.

- ## Inadequate preliminary investigations

  Under Article 108 of the old CPC, the procuracy is obliged to investigate when it learns of an alleged crime. Alternatively, the victims of a human rights violation or their relatives can file a complaint with a procurator's office. The procuracy then undertakes a preliminary investigation. If as a result of this investigation the procuracy determines that there is evidence of a crime, it should open a criminal investigation. Under Article 195 of the old CPC, this preliminary investigation may be suspended if it is not possible to identify the alleged perpetrator. If the procuracy receives information that there are additional facts, or if the victim or their relative is aware of steps, such as the interviewing of witnesses, that have not been taken, the procuracy must reactivate the investigation. There is no time limit for reopening a suspended investigation. The new CPC contains similar, though slightly strengthened, provisions. However, it is as yet unclear whether the new laws will be implemented more rigorously and so provide increased protection against torture or ill-treatment.

In practice, the informal preliminary inquiry has often proved not to be an effective or a "good faith" investigation into the facts. Amnesty International has information about numerous cases where the procuracy has dismissed the allegations, despite strong evidence that torture has taken place. According to reports, only a small percentage of complaints of torture and ill-treatment submitted to the procuracy reaches the courts. Most complaints are rejected by the procuracy at the initial, informal investigation stage. In cases where the alleged torturers have been charged, it has frequently been as a result of efforts by the victim and their lawyers over long periods to have the investigation reopened, often many times over.

One reason for the ineffectiveness of the preliminary inquiry and subsequent investigations has been the dual role of the procuracy, as provided for under the old CPC, which resulted in a conflict of interest. The procuracy was responsible for both prosecuting a person accused of a crime and investigating allegations that the accused had been tortured or ill-treated. If the procuracy determined that the accused had indeed been tortured or ill-treated, the same body risked undermining its own case. Under the new CPC, if the court determines there has been any breach of the code, then the evidence must be rejected. It remains to be seen whether this provision will work in practice and whether it will combat the practice of torture and ill-treatment.

- **Lack of independent medical examination**
  A key piece of evidence in cases of torture or ill-treatment is an accurate medical record of the injuries — physical and psychological — suffered. In Russia, victims of torture and ill-treatment face serious obstacles in having their injuries recorded by qualified medical personnel. One problem is that they are often denied access to independent medical professionals; another is that some of the torture techniques used, such as "*slonik*", do not leave physical traces.

  Russian courts are reluctant to accept medical reports other than those from state-run medical centres.

Under Article 184 of the old CPC, the investigator has the authority to order an official medical evaluation, including a psychological assessment, of a suspect. However, an investigator who may have been involved in coercion using torture and ill-treatment is unlikely to wish to have any physical or psychological injuries resulting from unlawful acts of law enforcement officers recorded by medical experts, which could render any testimony, including a "confession", subject to question.

Amnesty International is concerned that provisions of the new CPC compound the problem. Under Article 195, the investigator, having recognized that a medical examination is necessary, is to submit a request to the court. Disturbingly, the provision under the old CPC enabling the investigator to be present at such an examination is retained and indeed expanded in the new code. Although Article 197(2) states that the presence of the investigator "will be reflected in the conclusions of the [medical] expert", it is difficult to see how the presence of an investigator during a medical examination of an alleged torture victim could contribute to an effective examination of the victim, who may be reluctant to provide a full account of what happened or any resultant physical or psychological injuries.

The European Committee for the Prevention of Torture and Inhuman or Degrading Treatment or Punishment (CPT) has also stated that "all medical examinations of persons in custody are to be conducted out of the hearing and — unless the doctor concerned expressly requests otherwise in a given case — out of sight of police officers".[60]

- **Delays**
  Long delays in the procedures involved in bringing a complaint against torture or ill-treatment mean that by the time meaningful action is taken, forensic and other evidence has often become unavailable or been lost.

- **Corruption of evidence by police**

  It has been alleged that in some cases police officers accused of torture, or their colleagues, have destroyed or tampered with incriminating evidence.

- **Intimidation by police**

  In some cases, witnesses as well as lawyers pursuing complaints about torture and ill-treatment face intimidation and harassment by police.

- **Lack of availability of lawyers**

  There is a reported shortage of lawyers willing to represent victims of alleged torture or ill-treatment. Many victims of such human rights abuses cannot afford legal representation.

- **Lack of independent body to prosecute acts of torture**

  There is no independent body with powers (including the power to subpoena witnesses) to investigate and prosecute acts of torture and ill-treatment by law enforcement officials and members of the security forces. The current system leaves this function in the hands of the procuracy which, as stated above, results in a direct conflict of interest.

- **Lack of reparation**

  Reparation for the victims of torture and ill-treatment, including restitution, compensation and rehabilitation, remains theoretical in Russia, despite the country's ratification of international treaties that guarantee the rights of victims to effective redress and fair and adequate compensation.[61] In a system that largely fails to acknowledge, investigate and prosecute the perpetrators of torture and ill-treatment, the victims have little chance of receiving reparation.

  The Constitution guarantees compensation for victims of crime. The provisions are only partially in line with Article 14 of the Convention against Torture, which requires every state party to "ensure in its legal system that the victim of an act of torture obtains redress and has an enforceable right to fair and adequate compensation, including the means for as full rehabilitation as possible. In the event of the death of the victim as a result of an act of torture, his dependants shall be entitled to compensation". The fact that there is no specific reference in Russian law to rehabilitation for victims of torture and ill-treatment is a significant omission.

Victims of torture and ill-treatment can turn to a non-judicial mechanism of redress — the institution of the ombudsman. The role of the ombudsman is primarily to monitor actions by the president and his administration and to address complaints about maladministration from members of the public who have already exhausted available administrative and judicial remedies. The ombudsman is empowered to appeal to the federal Constitutional Court and initiate complaints concerning human rights violations that affect large numbers of people. Oleg Mironov, who was appointed federal Ombudsman for human rights in 1998, has been an outspoken critic of torture and ill-treatment in Russia, particularly in the penitentiary system.

In addition to the federal ombudsman, Russia's regions are permitted to establish regional parliamentary ombudsmen. As of mid-2002, 20 regions had established such offices. Although their mandates reportedly vary, each office investigates complaints against the regional administration and presents an annual report to the regional parliament. While initial reports suggest that several of these ombudsmen have taken positive steps in investigating such complaints, at the time of writing it was still unclear whether the authorities would act on their findings and introduce meaningful reforms.

In conclusion, the promised changes to the CPC address some of the factors that have fed the climate of impunity for torturers. However, as has been shown, the Constitution and provisions of Russian law already set out guarantees and mechanisms for respect of human rights that are internationally guaranteed. Yet these provisions, especially those pertaining to detainees in police custody, are simply ignored in practice. What is required is the political will to ensure prompt, independent, impartial and thorough investigations into each and every allegation of torture and ill-treatment, and prosecutions of those responsible — otherwise the abuses will continue.

Chapter 3: Abuses in Chechnya

"Still not found your husband? Then look for him in a pit!"

Advice given to Zura Mandykhadzhieva by a Russian soldier as she left her village to talk to Amnesty International delegates, November 2001

Zura Mandykhadzhieva told Amnesty International that at 3am on 6 November 2001, armed soldiers wearing masks and battle fatigues broke down the door to her home in the village of Tsotsin-Yurt, Kurchaloi district. Zura Mandykhadzhieva, her husband, Shamil Mandykhadzhiev, and their 16-year-old son, Imam, went downstairs to investigate. Zura Mandykhadzhieva stated that the soldiers knocked her son to the ground, hit her on the head, and forced all three to lie on the ground. She said Shamil Mandykhadzhiev was so severely beaten that blood started to seep from his ear. Zura Mandykhadzhieva begged the soldiers not to take her husband away. She said that one of the soldiers hit her on the head, leaving her dazed. Then she heard a soldier say, "On the count of three, I'm going to shoot". She heard two shots as her husband was shot in both legs.

Zura Mandykhadzhieva reported that before the soldiers left they set alight her brother's car, which was parked outside the house, and took her husband's passport. Zura Mandykhadzhieva took her husband to the local hospital for treatment. The following day, soldiers came to the hospital, along with the Russian military commandant of Kurchaloi district and the head of the Kurchaloi district state security service, the FSB.[62] Shamil Mandykhadzhiev was reportedly taken away on a stretcher to the local detention facility in a former flour mill at the edge of the village. Zura Mandykhadzhieva told Amnesty International that she brought food to the detention centre every day for six days. On the sixth day, an officer told her that her husband was still alive but that he had been taken away, possibly to a Temporary Department of Internal Affairs (VOVD)[63] detention facility in Kurchaloi. When she went there, officials told her to go to the Russian military base at Khankala.

However, there was no trace of Shamil Mandykhadzhiev there.

Zura Mandykhadzhieva

> The Kurchaloi procuracy opened a criminal investigation into Shamil Mandykhadzhiev's "disappearance" in response to a request by Zura Mandykhadzhieva. She still does not know where her husband is or what has happened to him.

The conflict in Chechnya has been characterized by serious violations of international human rights and humanitarian law. Independent verification of violations has frequently been gravely hampered by the security situation in the region, and obstacles to access imposed by the Russian authorities on international human rights monitors, as well as domestic and foreign journalists, seeking to operate in Chechnya. However, Amnesty International has actively researched numerous, consistent and credible reports that Russian forces have been responsible for widespread human rights violations such as "disappearances", extrajudicial executions and torture, including rape. These violations would be serious breaches of the Geneva Conventions, and constitute war crimes.

Chechen forces are also reported to have violated international humanitarian law, although independent investigation can likewise be very problematic. Chechen fighters who have been operating in and around populated areas have reportedly failed to take measures to protect civilians. According to reports, they have targeted civilian members of the pro-Moscow administration in attacks that have resulted in dozens of fatalities and serious injuries, and kidnapped civilians and held them hostage.[64] Chechen forces also claim to have executed captured members of the Russian armed forces.[65] Such abuses can also constitute war crimes.

Amnesty International has received numerous reports that Russian forces have looted private homes and forced civilians to hand over money and jewellery at gunpoint. In some reported cases, for example during an attack on the village of Katyr-Yurt in February 2000, the looting appears to have been highly organized, with a wide range of military vehicles, including trucks and helicopters reportedly used to take away private property. In other cases, Russian security forces are reported to have burned down or otherwise destroyed civilian homes in what appeared to be deliberate acts of reprisal.

Amnesty International is concerned that the authorities have failed to investigate allegations of violations by Russian forces adequately and to bring those responsible to justice. This has created a climate in which Russian security forces believe that they can continue to violate the fundamental rights of the civilian population in Chechnya with impunity.

Hundreds of thousands of people have fled their homes to escape the fighting. Most of those living in camps for displaced people in Chechnya and Ingushetia are women and children. Many of the camps visited by Amnesty International delegates are overcrowded and insanitary. Distribution of humanitarian aid from the state has been intermittent and arbitrarily withheld. Since December 1999, the Russian authorities have been notoriously reluctant to register new arrivals at these camps and others across Russia.[66] Without registration, a displaced person has no access to state-provided shelter, humanitarian aid, education or healthcare.

Background

The Republic of Chechnya is flanked by the Republics of Ingushetia and Dagestan on the southern border of the Russian Federation. It lies on the route of pipelines linking oil fields of the Caspian Sea to the port of Novorossiisk on the Black Sea.

In 1994, on the eve of the first conflict between Chechen and Russian forces, about a million people were believed to live in Chechnya. The impact of conflicts and instability has been to reduce dramatically the number of people living in the Republic.

Since the collapse of the Soviet Union in 1991, Chechnya has undergone two armed conflicts. Although estimates of the number of casualties sustained during the first conflict (1994 to 1996) vary widely, thousands of members of the Russian security forces, ethnic Chechen and Russian civilians and Chechen fighters are believed to have been killed.[67] Both sides are reported to have flouted international humanitarian law. The conflict ended in 1996 with a peace settlement that resulted in the complete withdrawal of Russian troops from Chechnya and agreement to determine the status of Chechnya within five years.[68]

© Heidi Bradner/Panos Pictures

In January 1997, Aslan Maskhadov emerged as the winner of presidential elections in Chechnya. The Organization for Security and Co-operation in Europe stated that these elections "represented the free will of those entitled to vote".[69]

A Russian soldier advancing down an isolated road in the Chechen countryside, 1999.

In the aftermath of the first conflict, the Russian authorities made little effort to investigate or prosecute those responsible for human rights violations. For example, the Russian Interior Ministry troops reportedly responsible for the killing of at least 103 civilians in the village of Samashki in April 1995 have never been brought to justice.[70]

The two years between the end of the first conflict and the beginning of the second were marked by a wholesale breakdown of law and order in Chechnya. Reports of kidnappings by gangs demanding ransoms were widespread and there were many reports that hostages were ill-treated and tortured. Some were raped. Several were killed. In June 1997 Chechen President Aslan Maskhadov announced the imposition of a version of *Shari'a* (Islamic law), reportedly in an attempt to address the growing incidence of kidnapping.[71] Under this law, the Chechen authorities carried out at least two public executions by firing squad in 1997.

In September 1999 Russian forces were once again sent to Chechnya. The Russian authorities claimed that the triggers for renewed conflict were an attack on several towns and villages in neighbouring Dagestan by up to 1,000 Chechen fighters, and a series of bombings of apartment buildings in Buinaksk, Volgodonsk and Moscow, which killed hundreds of people.[72] In the only case to come to trial, on 19 March 2001 a court in Dagestan convicted six men of the bombing in Buinaksk.[73] The Russian authorities blamed the other bombings on "Chechens".

Legal framework

Russia is obliged to respect all the international human rights instruments to which it is a party, such as the International Covenant on Civil and Political Rights (ICCPR) and the European Convention for the Protection of Human Rights and Fundamental Freedoms (see Chapter 1, International standards, for more details). However, there have been numerous reports that Russian forces are responsible for violating some of the rights guaranteed in these treaties, including the rights not to be subjected to arbitrary detention, torture, "disappearance" or extrajudicial execution.

Russia is also a state party to the four Geneva Conventions of 1949 and their two Additional Protocols of 1977, the second of which covers non-international armed conflict.

The Russian government has maintained that the second conflict in Chechnya is an "anti-terrorist operation", not an armed conflict. However, Article 1 of the 1977 Protocol II to the Geneva Conventions defines internal armed conflict as:

"[A]ll armed conflicts which are not covered by Article 1 of the Protocol Additional to the Geneva Conventions of 12 August 1949, and relating to the Protection of Victims of International Armed Conflicts (Protocol I) and which take place in the territory of a High Contracting Party between its armed forces and dissident armed forces or other organized armed groups which, **under responsible command, exercise such control over a part of its territory as to enable them to carry out sustained and concerted military operations and to implement this Protocol**." (Emphasis added.)

International humanitarian law as embodied in the four 1949 Geneva Conventions and Additional Protocol II, sets out minimum standards of conduct applicable to non-international armed conflict, such as that in Chechnya, and is aimed primarily at protecting civilians and those placed *hors de combat*, for example, prisoners and the wounded. In addition, Article 3 common to the four 1949 Geneva Conventions and their Additional Protocol II expressly prohibit the following acts or threats to commit such acts with respect to civilians and persons *hors de combat*:

- violence to the life, health and physical or mental well being of persons, in particular murder of all kinds, cruel treatment and torture; mutilation, or any form of corporal punishment;
- taking of hostages;
- outrages upon personal dignity, in particular, humiliating and degrading treatment, rape, and any form of indecent assault;
- the passing of sentences and the carrying out of executions without previous judgment pronounced by a regularly constituted court, affording all the judicial guarantees which are recognized as indispensable by civilized peoples;
- collective punishments;
- pillage.

States have a positive obligation or duty to investigate and prosecute members of its security forces for violations of international human rights and humanitarian law committed during armed conflict.74 The Russian state has a variety of legal mechanisms under which it can prosecute members of its forces for violations of international human rights and humanitarian law.

The international community

The record of the international community's response to human rights abuses in Chechnya is at best mixed. In 2000 and 2001 the UN Commission on Human Rights took unprecedented action in condemning the human rights situation in Chechnya.75 In particular, in 2001 it condemned the continued use of disproportionate and indiscriminate force by Russian military forces and other breaches of human rights and humanitarian law, as well as all attacks and breaches of international humanitarian law perpetrated by Chechen fighters. Both resolutions called on the Russian government to establish a national broad-based and independent commission of inquiry into alleged violations of human rights and international humanitarian law, and requested that the government extend invitations to visit Chechnya and neighbouring republics to five of the UN human rights mechanisms. These mechanisms[76] were to report their findings to the Commission and the General Assembly. The public response of the Russian Federation was a refusal to comply with these resolutions.[77]

Following the attacks in the USA on 11 September 2001, Russian claims that it was conducting an anti-terrorist operation in Chechnya found new resonance in the international community. International criticism of abuses in Chechnya has become more muted, apparently in response to Russian support for the US-led military intervention in Afghanistan and for US President George W. Bush's so-called "war on terrorism". Despite this, a draft resolution on the situation in Chechnya was proposed and debated during the Commission on Human Rights' session in 2002. However, in a statement made before the vote, a member of the Russian delegation urged all those who opposed "terrorism" to vote against the resolution. In the subsequent vote the draft resolution was narrowly defeated.

On a regional level, the Organization for Security and Co-operation in Europe has been working to promote the building of democratic institutions, respect for human rights and the rule of law, and a peaceful resolution to the conflict.

The Council of Europe, including its Secretary General, the European Committee for the Prevention of Torture and Inhuman or Degrading Treatment or Punishment (CPT), the Parliamentary Assembly and the Commissioner for Human Rights have been monitoring the human rights situation in the Russian Federation, and in Chechnya in particular. The latter two of these bodies have been critical of the conduct of the Russian forces and Chechen fighters. They have urged both sides to respect human rights and are continuing efforts to mediate a political solution. In a recommendation published on 30 May 2002, the Council of

Europe's Commissioner for Human Rights, Alvaro Gil-Robles, raised continuing concern about the Russian security forces' conduct during raids in Chechen towns and villages. He stated that "some of these operations have resulted in substantial unjustified acts of violence by soldiers against the civilian population". He also raised concern about "disappearances", and noted that "the continuing disappearances engender a strong feeling of fear, vulnerability and uneasiness among civilians vis-a-vis the federal forces". Concern was also raised about the failure to fully implement measures aimed at ensuring respect for human rights by the security forces. He made five specific recommendations, aimed at ensuring that the Russian authorities more vigorously implement provisions governing the conduct of the security forces in Chechnya and take steps to facilitate investigations into human rights violations.[78]

The current conflict

> *"[The] centre of the city [Grozny] has been totally and systematically destroyed. We did not see a single building intact."*
> Lord Judd, member of the Political Affairs Committee of the Parliamentary Assembly of the Council of Europe, April 2000[79]

On 7 October 2001 Russian forces surrounded the village of Tsotsin-Yurt in preparation for a house-by-house raid of the village the following day. One villager, Amkhat Vakhaev, told Amnesty International that he could hear the screams of his neighbour, Aset Artsoeva, as soldiers beat her husband, Aiub Artsoev, and their 15-year-old son. A soldier reportedly beat Aset Artsoeva on the back of her head with a rifle butt. As she lay unconscious, the soldiers took her husband away.

Aset Artsoeva, Amkhat Vakhaev and other neighbours began to gather outside the house. They approached the soldiers to ask why they had taken Aiub Artsoev. The soldiers warned them not to come any nearer or they would open fire. The group of villagers apparently ignored this warning and one of the soldiers opened fire. Amkhat Vakhaev said that his 25-year-old wife, Birlant Dzhonalieva, who was carrying their seven-month-old baby in her arms, was hit in the stomach and

© Thomas Dworzak/Magnum Photos

A boy stands in front of the ruins of a house in Urus-Martan which was reportedly destroyed during an air raid by Russian planes in which eight people were killed. October 1999.

seriously wounded. Amkhat Vakhaev's 15-year-old cousin, Kheda Artsoeva, was also injured.

About two days later Aiub Artsoev was found alive, but badly injured, by a villager in a field where he had apparently been left by soldiers. He was covered in bruises and both his arms and several ribs were reportedly broken as a result of beatings. The soldiers had apparently taken him to a field between the villages of Kurchaloi and Mairtup and tortured him in an attempt to force him to "admit" that he had guns in his home. Amkhat Vakhaev stated that the soldiers beat Aiub Artsoev and subjected him to electro-shock torture; they made cuts on both of his legs and inserted live electrical wires.

To Amnesty International's knowledge no investigation has ever been carried out into these allegations of torture or into the other abuses reported to have taken place during the repeated raids by Russian forces on Tsotsin-Yurt. These raids have reportedly left at least three people dead and resulted in the "disappearance" of at least 20 villagers.

Russian armed forces have subjected towns and villages in Chechnya to artillery, rocket and air attacks that have caused massive destruction, particularly in Grozny but also in other areas such as the village of Komsomolskoe. Lord Judd, member of the Political Affairs Committee of the Parliamentary

Assembly of the Council of Europe, visited Grozny in early 2000 with members of a Council of Europe *ad hoc* committee on Chechnya. While acknowledging that the city had suffered damage during the first Chechnya conflict, Lord Judd wrote that "the current level of destruction suggests that Grozny has been the target of indiscriminate, disproportionate bombardment by the Russian forces."[80]

There have been many reported cases where Russian forces did not give the civilian population prior warning of the bombardment or facilitate their evacuation from the area. Indeed, there have been instances — for example in Grozny (January 2000), Katyr-Yurt (February 2000) and Komsomolskoe (March 2000) — where Russian forces are reported to have actively prevented civilians from leaving the combat area, or fired on the exit routes.[81]

Typically, artillery and aerial bombardments by Russian forces are followed by raids (known as *zachistka*, meaning "clean-up" or "mop-up") ostensibly aimed at locating and engaging any remaining Chechen fighters. Many of the violations of human rights and international humanitarian law committed by Russian security forces in Chechnya take place in the context of such raids, which have continued unabated throughout the current conflict.[82] In some cases, Russian forces have returned over and over again to the same village to carry out raids characterized by indiscriminate violence and abuse of civilians.[83]

It is often difficult to determine precisely which security force units are responsible for a particular raid. The Russian authorities have deployed a wide variety of forces in Chechnya. These include federal soldiers of the Russian army, among them conscripts, who are under the control of the Ministry of Defence. There are also several forces under the control of the Interior Ministry, including special riot police, known as OMON,[84] and the state security service, the FSB. In addition, Russian forces also include "contract" soldiers — volunteers who agree to serve in Chechnya under time-limited contracts in exchange for payment.[85] Often, the men in these units are serving policemen or retired soldiers.

According to reports, combinations of federal soldiers, OMON officers and FSB personnel are often involved in raids. Other sub-units of special federal and Interior Ministry forces, known as "*Spetsnaz*", are also believed to take part. Some security force units reportedly black out identifying information on their vehicles during raids.

Torture

"I thought it would be better to die quickly to escape the pain."
Alaudin Sadykov, speaking to Amnesty International about his treatment in detention

Alaudin Sadykov, a 51-year-old schoolteacher from Grozny, remained in the city during the latest conflict to assist in the distribution of humanitarian aid.

He told Amnesty International that he was detained by OMON officers on 5 March 2000 and taken to the VOVD police station in the Oktiabrskii district of Grozny. There he was reportedly beaten, forced to eat his own hair, and burned with red-hot pieces of metal; burn scars on his hands are still visible. One of the men allegedly told Alaudin Sadykov that he wouldn't leave the police station alive. Alaudin Sadykov said that, following a prolonged beating, he was dragged to a cellar where up to six men used him like a "live football", breaking his teeth and ribs and kicking him until he lost consciousness.

Later that day, the officers reportedly took Alaudin Sadykov back to his home and looted it. They then took him back to the police station, accusing him of having explosives in his home and blowing up a house, and subjected him to a prolonged beating using rifle butts. Alaudin Sadykov said that four days later, men in battle fatigues again beat him and cut off his ear.[86] He told Amnesty International:

"They beat me again and said, 'Let's cut off his head'. They took a large knife for slaughtering animals and cut off my left ear completely. Then they said, 'We'll cut your head off later'. While I

© Paula Allen

was lying on the floor, there was blood every-where and my ear was lying next to me. Then one of the men who was guarding me came in and photographed me lying there. He and the others were from Khanty-Mansiiskii Region police, OMON."

Alaudin Sadykov (centre) and (inset) displaying the left side of his face where his ear was severed.

Alaudin Sadykov was released on 24 May 2000. An investigation into the case, which focused solely on the beatings, was opened on 13 July 2000. This investigation was later suspended on the grounds that the perpetrator could not be identified. To Amnesty International's knowledge, no other investigation has been carried out into Alaudin Sadykov's allegations of torture.

Alaudin Sadykov's case is one of those which is being pursued by the non-governmental organization, Chechnya Justice Initiative (CJI). The CJI, which was set up in 2001 by human rights activists and lawyers, has submitted over 30 cases to the European Court of Human Rights concerning allegations of human rights violations in Chechnya including torture, "disappearance", and extrajudicial execution. As of mid-2002, the European Court had yet to rule on the admissibility of these cases.

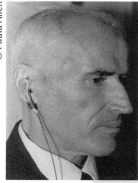

© Paula Allen

Zaindi Bisultanov, shown with the hearing aid he must now wear.

"I cannot exclude the possibility that they will come and get me again at any time, in the night from my bed, as they did before. I don't know when it is going to happen, but I'm waiting. When I see federal soldiers now my body starts to shake. It's fear, real fear." Zaindi Bisultanov

Zaindi Bisultanov, a 55-year-old lawyer, told Amnesty International that he was woken on 5 June 2000 at the home of relatives in Grozny by Russian federal soldiers wearing masks. He said that the soldiers placed a sack over his head, took him to a waiting car and then drove a short distance before dragging him out of the car, putting him against a wall and beating him on the chest and back. Zaindi Bisultanov stated that he was then put back in the car and driven to the outskirts of Grozny to a village called Dachnyi Poselok, not far from the main Russian military base in Khankala, where he was beaten and kicked.

"They beat me about the head and heart when I was kneeling. I was sitting with my left side towards them. They kicked me in the left ear. That ear is now basically useless, the nerves are damaged."

Zaindi Bisultanov told Amnesty International that his hands were then tied behind his back in a painful raised position with a rope that cut into his skin. He said he was taken to a basement, with the sack still over his head, where three other men were also held, two of whom he later learned were his relatives, the brothers Leche and Said-Emin Tisaev. The third man was reportedly named Khusein, from Gudermes. Zaindi Bisultanov stated that the four men were sealed into the basement by a concrete slab which was placed over the entrance by guards who then abandoned them. Zaindi Bisultanov believes that the soldiers intended that they should die entombed in the basement, but the men managed to untie their hands and escape.

"It was hard for me to walk — I had been beaten severely in the genital area. If I was sitting, I couldn't stand up, if I was standing, I couldn't sit down. It was unbearably painful. We were badly beaten."

Eventually, the men were found by relatives who hid them. Too afraid to seek medical help officially, Zaindi Bisultanov did not file a written complaint with the Grozny procuracy until October 2001. Amnesty International is not aware of any prosecution brought by the authorities in connection with the alleged torture of Zaindi Bisultanov.

There have been persistent and credible reports of widespread torture and ill-treatment by Russian forces in Chechnya. Thousands of civilians have been detained for varying periods during military raids or document checks. Although men between the ages of 18 and 30 are most likely to be picked up, women and children have also been detained. In some cases, detainees have reportedly been held in squalid facilities that amounted to little more than pits in the ground beside a checkpoint or at the main Russian military base at Khankala. Many of those detained have been tortured or ill-treated.[87]

Methods of torture used by Russian forces that Amnesty International has documented include: rape of men, women and children; electric shocks; prolonged beatings, including on the genitals and on the ears causing damage to hearing or deafness; amputation of ears and fingers; and prolonged and painful shackling.

Because men and boys have frequently been arbitrarily detained by Russian forces following raids, many flee the area when they fear that their town or village may be raided; their families generally remain in their homes. Amnesty International has received several reports of women who remained in the village or town during raids being raped by Russian soldiers. The organization believes that the true extent of sexual abuse may be hidden. Women are often extremely reluctant to report rape because of the dysfunctional justice system (see below, Obstacles to justice) and because of the social stigma associated with rape.

According to witnesses, Zainap (not her real name) was eight months pregnant when she was raped in October 2001. Russian soldiers came to her home in the village of Kurchaloi intending to detain her husband. When they did not find him, they allegedly detained Zainap and took her to the VOVD at the military command post in Kurchaloi. Two women who were detained along with Zainap stated that she was repeatedly gang-raped and ill-treated by Russian soldiers and suffered a miscarriage. Zainap was released in mid-November, reportedly in exchange for 10 machine guns handed over by her relatives. Zainap reportedly underwent surgery after her release. Her husband reportedly refused to take her back because she had been raped.[88]

Amnesty International is concerned that the failure of the Russian authorities to issue clear messages that torture and ill-treatment by or with the consent or acquiescence of any member of its security forces will not be tolerated; to back this up by ensuring that reports of torture and ill-treatment are the subject of prompt, independent, impartial and thorough investigations; and to ensure that the perpetrators are brought to justice in the course of fair trials, has contributed in large part to the prevalence and persistence of this pattern of abuse.

Relatives of the "disappeared" try to identify the bodies of their loved ones in a building in central Grozny, February 2001. Fifty-one bodies were discovered in the village of Dachnyi Poselok, near the Russian military base at Khankala, many reportedly bearing signs of torture and mutilation.

Extrajudicial executions

The largely abandoned village of Dachnyi Poselok lies around 500m from the main Russian military base at Khankala. In February 2001, following rumours about the discovery of bodies at the village, relatives searching for their "disappeared" loved ones discovered 51 bodies in or around abandoned houses

©Human Rights Centre Memorial

63

in Dachnyi Poselok. The bodies had been dumped at various points in the village; many had their hands bound and reportedly bore the signs of torture and mutilation. Prompt action by the Russian human rights organization Memorial prevented the bodies from being swiftly buried by Russian troops. The discovery of these bodies, so close to a major military base, strongly suggests Russian forces involvement in the killings and is consistent with the many reports received by Amnesty International of extrajudicial executions of Chechen civilians and captured fighters by Russian security forces.

Most extrajudicial executions appear to have involved the widespread and deliberate killing of individual civilians or captured fighters. However, mass killings of civilians have also been reported, particularly in the context of bouts of intense military activity, such as the battle for Grozny in January 2000. Three mass killings of civilians were reportedly carried out by Russian forces between December 1999 and February 2000 in which at least 112 civilians were killed. The first took place in the village of Alkhan-Yurt, approximately 15km southwest of Grozny; the second was carried out in the Staropromyslovskii district in northwest Grozny; and the third and largest occurred in the Aldi district in southern Grozny. Russian soldiers also reportedly raped civilians during these attacks and looted and burned down homes.[90]

'Disappearances'

Twenty-four-year-old Zelimkhan Murdalov left his home in Grozny on 2 January 2001, saying he would be back in an hour. That was the last his family ever saw of him.

When Zelimkhan Murdalov failed to return, his father, Astemir Murdalov, went to the Leninskii military command post to look for him. Two women waiting outside the post for news of their relatives told him that a young man matching his son's description had been detained near Minutka Square in the centre of the city. Astemir Murdalov went to the police station in Minutka Square where the deputy head told him that his son was being held at the police station on charges of possessing cannabis and that they were waiting for a lawyer to come in order to release him.

© Paula Allen

Astemir Murdalov | Astemir Murdalov left to find a lawyer. When he returned to the police station he was reportedly not allowed to enter. For two days the family and neighbours waited outside the police station in vain. On 5 January 2001, Astemir Murdalov went to the Grozny procuracy. Accompanied by the city procurator and the city commandant, Astemir Murdalov reportedly went back to the police station where staff claimed that Zelimkhan Murdalov had been released earlier that morning.

According to reports, detainees who had been held in the same cell as Zelimkhan Murdalov told the procurator that when they saw him on 3 January 2001 he was unconscious; his arm was broken and the bone was protruding from the skin; his genitals had been torn off; and his ear had been severed. A doctor reportedly said he had treated Zelimkhan Murdalov that night, but stated that his wounds were light; that the ear was torn, not severed; and that the injuries had been sustained in a fall.

On 7 January 2001 a criminal investigation was opened into Zelimkhan Murdalov's "disappearance". In January 2002 an officer was arrested, reportedly in connection with the treatment of Zelimkhan Murdalov in detention. At the time of writing the officer had not yet been brought to trial and no one, to Amnesty International's knowledge, had been charged in connection with Zelimkhan Murdalov's "disappearance".

Astemir Murdalov still does not know the fate or whereabouts of his son.

Hundreds of people are believed to have "disappeared" at the hands of Russian security forces in Chechnya since the start of the second conflict in 1999.[91] The reluctance of the authorities to provide statistical information about abuses in Chechnya and the lack of access to the region afforded to independent human rights monitors make it difficult to assess the scale of this abuse and the true number of "disappearances" may well be much higher.[92]

Many of the victims are feared to have been killed, often after being tortured. For the close relatives left behind, the "disappearance" of a loved one can also amount to torture or cruel, inhuman or degrading treatment or punishment. They often have to face the uncertainty of not knowing what has happened to their relative after he or she was seen in the custody of the security forces, while their attempts to discover his or her fate and whereabouts are met with a lack of responsiveness on the part of the authorities.[93]

Obstacles to justice

> *"When I asked people in [the villages of] Yalkhoi-Mokhk, in Akhkinchu-Borzoe, 'Why don't you lodge formal complaints [with the authorities]?' they answered: 'Let them come to us. We are afraid... we are even afraid of you'... When I spoke about this with Terent'ev, the head of the Kurchaloi district commandant's office, he answered very rudely. I said to him, 'People are asking you to come to Yalkhoi-Mokhk'... I can't give you his answer, what he said to me in reply."*
> Natalia Estamirova, a member of the human rights organization Memorial working in Chechnya, January 2002[94]

Eighteen-year-old Kheda (Elza) Kungaeva was abducted from her family home in the village of Tangi-Chu on 26 March 2000 by Russian soldiers under the command of Colonel Yury Budanov. Colonel Budanov then took Kheda Kungaeva to his tent and strangled her. An official post-mortem, examined by Amnesty International, carried out by a Ministry of Defence pathologist, concluded that Kheda Kungaeva had been raped before her death. However, this finding has been ignored by the prosecution which charged Colonel Budanov with murder and abuse of power, but has failed to charge anyone with rape.

On 30 March 2000 Colonel Budanov was arrested. It was

The parents of Kheda (Elza) Kungaeva show photographs of their daughter taken before and after she was abducted and killed by Colonel Budanov.

widely reported that in the course of the investigation Colonel Budanov had admitted killing Kheda Kungaeva, but had stated that he strangled her during interrogation in a state of "temporary insanity". According to reports, Colonel Budanov underwent several psychiatric examinations during the course of the trial. One examination, conducted by the state-run Serbsky Institute in September 2001, supported his claim of temporary insanity. This finding means that, if convicted, he could receive a greatly reduced sentence.[95]

As of mid-2002 Colonel Budanov was the highest ranking officer to be charged with a serious crime during the second Chechnya conflict. However, even though Colonel Budanov has admitted killing Kheda Kungaeva, he still enjoys public and military support. For example, during the first week of his trial, which began on 28 February 2001, General Vladimir Shamanov came to the court to shake hands with Colonel Budanov.[96] This attitude is indicative of the huge obstacles faced by victims of grave human rights violations and their relatives in gaining justice and any form of redress.

In addition to the overriding problem of lack of political will on the part of the authorities to see Russian security forces prosecuted for human rights violations, there are many reasons why investigations and prosecutions in connection with violations in Chechnya have proved so inadequate.

- In the Russian Federation, there are two prosecutorial bodies that deal with crimes. The military procuracy investigates crimes committed by members of the Russian military, including sub-units and special units within the army. The civilian procuracy deals with crimes committed by civilians and forces under the control of the Interior Ministry, such as combat units, OMON officers, and other police and law enforcement bodies. When a formal complaint about a crime in Chechnya is lodged, the authorities have to determine which procuracy should deal with it. This is especially problematic as security forces regularly operate in mixed units involving Interior Ministry troops, OMON officers, "contract" soldiers and regular army units. This situation has meant that the procuracies have passed complaints from one to the other, resulting in protracted and frequently dysfunctional processes.
- Another cause of confusion and delay is the fact that civilians cannot appeal directly to the military procuracy, since these are located on military bases to which civilians do not have access. In cases where Russian army units are believed to be responsible for a crime, the victim must turn first to the civilian procuracy, which will then forward the complaint on to its counterpart in the military procuracy.
- The situation in Chechnya continues to pose considerable dangers for Russian officials. There is little incentive for investigators from the procuracy to travel to or within the region to investigate alleged crimes when their lives and security are at risk. According to one report, five representatives of the procuracy were killed in Chechnya in 2000.[97]
- Victims of human rights violations are afraid to complain — fear is perhaps the biggest obstacle to Chechens lodging formal complaints with the Russian authorities. Those who seek to file complaints with the authorities are fearful that

At 4am on 9 November 2001, masked Russian soldiers raided a house in Serzhen-Yurt in which five girls and two women were sleeping. The two women — Aset Yakhiaeva (also known as "Zargan"), aged 45, and Milana Betirgirieva (also known as "Ainat"), aged 21 — were staying in the village to help with preparations for the wedding of a neighbour's daughter.

According to witnesses, the soldiers cut the electricity to the house. When the terrified girls began to cry, the soldiers threatened to shoot them if they did not keep quiet. The soldiers then shone torches into the girls' faces and threatened to rape them. One of the girls told Amnesty International that an officer entered the room and ordered the soldiers not to touch them. The soldiers then searched the house, demanding money and threatening to kill the girls.

After the soldiers left, the girls went to the room in which Aset Yakhiaeva and Milana Betirgirieva had been sleeping. The room was empty. In the street, the girls found some of the women's clothes, including Milana Betirgirieva's skirt and a blouse. There has been no further information as to the fate and whereabouts of the two women.

The manner in which Aset Yakhiaeva and Milana Betirgirieva were apparently taken away is consistent with other reported incidents where people have been detained by Russian forces.

Amnesty International is continuing to investigate the circumstances surrounding the "disappearance" of Aset Yakhiaeva and Milana Betirgirieva and is gravely concerned for their welfare.[98]

this may entail negative consequences, including threats and intimidation from the units responsible for the violation. Moreover, travelling within Chechnya to file a complaint with the authorities entails risk; even a relatively short journey within Chechnya involves passing through innumerable checkpoints, each an opportunity for the extortion of bribes, arbitrary detention and other forms of abuse.

Since Russia ratified the European Convention for the Protection of Human Rights and Fundamental Freedoms in 1998, people who claim that their rights under the Convention have been violated may take their case to the European Court of Human Rights in Strasbourg. In order for complaints alleging violations of rights under the Convention to be considered admissible, the complainant must first exhaust available domestic legal remedies in the form of the national court system and the case must be filed with the European Court of Human Rights within six months. Because of the obstacles to filing complaints and the dysfunctional nature of the judicial system within Chechnya, some applicants to the European Court of Human Rights have reportedly complained that the available domestic legal remedies are ineffective. By mid-2002, a number of cases involving alleged human rights violations committed during the conflict in Chechnya had been filed with the European Court of Human Rights.

Lack of accountability

> *"Despite strong evidence of rape and other sexual violence committed by Russian forces in Chechnya, the Government of the Russian Federation has failed to conduct the necessary investigations or to hold anyone accountable for the vast majority of cases. To date, only one of the alleged perpetrators, a Russian tank commander, has been arrested and charged with sexual assault."*
> UN Special Rapporteur on violence against women, January 2001[99]

The Russian authorities have failed to take effective measures to address human rights violations committed by Russian security forces in Chechnya, including by guards in detention facilities. Amnesty International is concerned that these failures may be contributing to a climate in which Russian security forces believe that they can commit such abuses with impunity.

The measures which the authorities have taken to address human rights violations committed by Russian security forces during raids do not appear to have improved the conduct of Russian troops nor increased accountability for human rights violations. At the heart of this failure appears to be a lack of political will.

© Reuters

Chechen detainees walk in the yard of the Chernokozovo detention facility, watched by an officer from the Russian Interior Ministry, 28 February 2000.

The Russian authorities' responses to abuses have ranged from blanket denials of responsibility — for example, asserting that violations were in fact committed by Chechen fighters wearing Russian military uniforms — to an acknowledgement that violations have been committed by their forces, followed by inadequate measures to tackle the problem.

For example, Order No. 80 was introduced in March 2002. Although it requires investigations and prosecutions in connection with incidents of pillage, it does not call for such steps to be taken in response to reports of violations of the right to life and personal integrity by members of the Russian security forces, such as extrajudicial executions, "disappearances", and torture, including rape.

The order prohibits the security forces from wearing masks and concealing the identity of their units unless there is a valid "operational" reason for doing so, although it is unclear what such a reason might be. The order also requires Interior Ministry forces and police to announce their name, rank and purpose when entering civilian homes, but does not make this a requirement for federal soldiers or other units who often participate in these raids. These measures, then, even if fully

© AI (David Lothian)

Russian journalist Anna Politkovskaya receives the Global Award for Human Rights Journalism at the Amnesty International United Kingdom Media Awards 2001, for her investigation of a "filtration camp" where Russian troops reportedly held Chechen prisoners for ransom.

implemented, are not sufficient to bring about a meaningful increase in the accountability of Russian forces in Chechnya for human rights violations.

The head of the pro-Moscow administration in Chechnya, Akhmad Kadyrov, reportedly attacked Order No. 80 for failing to address violations during raids. He said, "People still disappear without a trace... those involved in the operations do not introduce themselves or say where those arrested are to be moved or what the charges against them are."[100]

Similarly, Decree No. 46, which was issued on 25 July 2001 by the General Procurator for the Russian Federation, states that procurators and representatives of local authorities should be present during military raids by Russian forces in Chechnya. The decree also requires Russian forces to inform the relatives when someone is detained and to record the time and place of detention. However, in practice these provisions are ineffective. For example, during a raid on Tsotsin-Yurt on

30 December 2001, military prosecutors were apparently present. However, at the time of writing, Amnesty International was not aware of any prosecutions having been brought in connection with the reported extrajudicial execution, "disappearance" or torture of civilians in Tsotsin-Yurt resulting from the raid.[101]

One consequence of the failure to hold Russian forces to account for their actions is that the civilian population in Chechnya remains deeply suspicious of the authorities and has little faith that any complaint that they bring will result in a prosecution. Indeed, reluctance to report violations is exacerbated by the very real fear that any interaction with the authorities could lead to detention, torture and ill-treatment.

Musa (not his real name) was detained in the village of Znamenskoe and brought to Chernokozovo in January 2000. Musa said that on 18 January 2000[102] he and other detainees were forced to walk along a line of about 20 masked men who beat them with clubs and hammers. He said that he sustained a fractured spine as a result of being beaten on his back with hammers. He was released on 5 February 2000 after his mother paid the 4,000 rubles reportedly demanded by the detention facility authorities.

Musa stated that he knew of several detainees, including children, who had been raped by guards at Chernokozovo. He said that he shared a cell with a 16-year-old boy who was beaten and raped and whose ear had been cut off by prison guards. Musa also said that soldiers had burned the hands of another cellmate with cigarette lighters and used a metal file to saw off the teeth of a 17-year-old boy also held in the cell.

Between December 1999 and January 2000, Amnesty International received numerous reports that detainees held at the Chernokozovo detention facility were subjected to torture and ill-treatment. During this period children, women and men were subjected to unrelenting violence from the moment they arrived at the facility; several detainees are known to have died following prolonged beatings.

Since 1998 the CPT has made nine visits to places where people have been deprived of their liberty by the Russian authorities. Five of these visits were to Chechnya. To date, the

Russian authorities have not authorized the release of the CPT's reports of its visits which include, among other things, recommendations aiming to prevent torture and ill-treatment.

In July 2001, the CPT took the extraordinary measure of issuing a public statement in which it raised concern about the failure of the government to investigate allegations of torture and ill-treatment at the Chernokozovo detention facility between December 1999 and January 2000. The CPT described the denial by the Russian authorities that there ever was such a facility during that period, as "clearly untenable and constitutes a failure to cooperate with the CPT".[103] To Amnesty International's knowledge no one has yet been brought to justice in connection with the torture or ill-treatment of detainees held in Chernokozovo between December 1999 and January 2000.

The CPT wrote to the Russian authorities on 10 May 2001 asking them to detail actions taken to counter the "climate of fear" in Chechnya among victims of torture and ill-treatment at the hands of the authorities and to encourage victims to come forward and register complaints. However, the CPT noted in its July 2001 statement that "the Russian authorities indicate that they are not willing to provide the information requested or to engage in a discussion with the CPT on their request."

> *"It is axiomatic that one of the most effective means of preventing ill-treatment of persons deprived of their liberty lies in the diligent examination by the relevant authorities of all complaints of such treatment brought before them and, where appropriate, the imposition of a suitable penalty. This will have a very strong deterrent effect. Conversely, if the relevant authorities do not take effective action upon complaints referred to them, those minded to ill-treat persons deprived of their liberty will quickly come to believe that they can act with impunity."*
>
> CPT, public statement concerning the Chechen Republic of the Russian Federation, July 2001

In April 2002 the Council of Europe Joint Working Group on Chechnya published a report that included recent statistics on the status of investigations and prosecutions throughout the current armed conflict.[104] The report states that there have been only three convictions for crimes committed by Russian security forces against civilians covered by the civilian procuracy; the report does not detail the charges. Although the report does not record any convictions of Russian security forces for crimes against civilians which come under the jurisdiction of the military procuracy, it notes that 43 cases have been referred to the military courts; 11 involve murder and two allegations of rape.

The Russian authorities have an obligation to respect, protect, ensure and promote fundamental human rights. They are clearly failing to fulfil this obligation to the civilian population of Chechnya. Those whose rights have been abused have a right to see justice done, to receive reparation and to see the wrongs done to them acknowledged and those responsible brought to justice. The Russian authorities are denying them this right. Amnesty International is calling on the authorities to live up to their obligations under national and international human rights and humanitarian law and to take concrete steps to prevent future abuses and to ensure effective redress and reparations for violations which have occurred in the past.

Recommendations

Amnesty International believes that the following measures would radically improve the protection of human rights in the Russian Federation. It calls on the Russian authorities to:

1. Show a clear political commitment to promote and protect fundamental human rights for everybody and to give an unequivocal message that violations of these rights will not be tolerated.

2. Take immediate and concrete steps towards the abolition of the death penalty in law and ratify Protocols No. 6 and 13 to the European Convention for the Protection of Human Rights and Fundamental Freedoms and the Second Optional Protocol to the International Covenant on Civil and Political Rights aiming at the abolition of the death penalty.

3. Institute training and monitoring programs to ensure that law enforcement and other officials do not act in a discriminatory way towards people on the basis of their gender, sexual orientation, ethnic or national origin or any other aspects of their identity or status.

4. Make domestic violence a distinct criminal offence, and introduce training for law enforcement officials to recognize and prosecute violence against women, including domestic violence and trafficking of women.

5. Ratify the Optional Protocol to the Convention on the Elimination of All Forms of Discrimination against Women, granting authority to the Committee on the Elimination of Discrimination against Women (CEDAW) to examine complaints by individuals and groups.

6. Ensure that children are deprived of their liberty only as a measure of last resort and for the shortest appropriate time.

7. Review legislation and regulations at federal and regional levels with the aim of removing all elements of the passport and registration system (formerly known as the "*propiska*" system) which serve as a basis for systematic discrimination.

Two children at Sleptsovsk refugee camp, Ingushetia, March 2002. More than 200,000 people have been displaced during the two conflicts in Chechnya, the majority of them women and children.

8. Ensure that crimes that are racially motivated are classified and prosecuted as such.

9. Establish national laws and procedures consistent with the Organization for Security and Co-operation in Europe (OSCE) Principles Governing Conventional Arms Transfers (agreed in November 1993) to prevent exports of arms and security equipment and technology where there is a danger that those exports will be used for serious violations of international human rights and humanitarian law.

Torture and ill-treatment

10. Adopt a law which specifically criminalizes torture and ill-treatment in line with international human rights standards — including Article 1 of the Convention against Torture — and which provides for penalties that take into account the grave nature of these offences.

11. Implement in practice the prohibition of coercion under Article 302 of the Criminal Code and ensure that Article 9 of the new Criminal Procedure Code (CPC), which prohibits anyone involved in criminal proceedings from being subjected to violence, torture or other cruel, inhuman or degrading treatment, is respected.

12. Ensure that prompt, impartial, independent and thorough investigations of complaints of torture are carried out and that the perpetrators are brought to justice in line with international human rights standards.

13. Establish an independent body with powers, including the power to subpoena witnesses, to investigate and prosecute acts of torture and ill-treatment by officials or that occur as a result of the acquiescence, instigation or consent of officials.

14. Ensure that all law enforcement personnel are trained in international law on the prohibition of torture and ill-treatment in all circumstances and are informed of the criminal liability that the use of torture and ill-treatment entails, regardless of rank.

15. Ensure that all detainees are guaranteed prompt access to a lawyer following arrest, as stipulated in the Russian Constitution. This right should be extended to anyone

summoned to a police station as a witness who is then questioned as a possible suspect.

16. Ensure that all evidence, including statements, admitted in any proceedings have been lawfully obtained.

17. Ensure that all detainees who allege that they were subjected to torture or ill-treatment are examined as a matter of routine by qualified and independent medical personnel for physical and psychological signs of torture.

18. Ensure that health care professionals at official treatment centres are trained in the recognition and treatment of injuries, including psychological, relating to torture and ill-treatment.

19. Amend the new CPC to ensure that medical reports from all qualified medical personnel are accepted as evidence in cases relating to allegations of torture and ill-treatment.

20. Ensure that female security personnel are present during the interrogation of women detainees and are solely responsible for conducting body searches of women detainees. There should be no contact between male guards and female prisoners without the presence of a female guard.

21. Include gender-specific information in programs to educate, inform and train relevant officials regarding the prohibition of torture.

22. Ensure that victims of human rights violations, including torture and ill-treatment, have access to reparation, including compensation, medical care and rehabilitation.

23. Introduce training for all law enforcement officials and members of the security forces on the special needs and rights of children, as set out in the Convention on the Rights of the Child.

24. Urgently address the causes of overcrowding in detention, particularly in pre-trial detention facilities, including through the implementation of new provisions under the new CPC that place greater emphasis on alternatives to pre-trial detention.

25. Authorize, without delay, publication of all reports of European Committee for the Prevention of Torture and Inhuman or Degrading Treatment or Punishment (CPT) visits to the Russian Federation, and translate and disseminate them widely in all relevant languages. Take all necessary

measures to implement the recommendations of the CPT without delay.

26. Take all other measures necessary to prevent and punish torture including those set out in Amnesty International's 12-Point Program for the Prevention of Torture by Agents of the State (Appendix 1).

Chechnya

Amnesty International calls on the government of the Russian Federation to implement the following recommendations in relation to the conduct of its forces in Chechnya:

27. Take urgent steps to ensure that civilians are protected at all times from the impact of security force operations.

28. Hold comprehensive and impartial investigations into allegations of violations of international human rights and humanitarian law, including war crimes, and bring those responsible to justice in accordance with international standards.

29. Ensure that all victims of violations of international human rights and humanitarian law have access to a system of effective redress and an enforceable right to fair and adequate reparation.

30. Take steps to build confidence between the civilian population and the authorities, including the appointment of trained, experienced and qualified mixed-gender teams of investigators and prosecutors to investigate allegations of torture involving sexual violence and rape against the civilian population.

31. Revise the training, disciplinary procedures and rules of engagement for the security forces, to prevent human rights violations.

32. Ensure that Order 80 and Decree 46 are expanded to cover all Russian security forces, including federal soldiers, involved in carrying out raids and that appropriate measures are taken against those who violate them.

33. Make available regularly up-to-date lists of all members of the Russian security forces charged and prosecuted for human rights violations committed in Chechnya, which

should include specific information on who has been charged with what crime. The list should also include information on the status of all investigations into and prosecutions in connection with violations of international human rights and humanitarian law in Chechnya.

34. Take all other measures necessary to prevent and punish torture including those set out in Amnesty International's 14-Point Program for the Prevention of Extrajudicial Executions (Appendix 2).

35. Carry out autopsies where there are grounds to believe the person may have died as a result of torture or extrajudicial execution, in order to determine the cause of death, whether injuries occurred prior to death and — where necessary — to establish the identity of the deceased.

36. Extend an invitation to and arrange without delay dates for visits of the UN Special Rapporteur on torture and the UN Special Rapporteur on extrajudicial, summary or arbitrary executions. Grant unrestricted access to Chechnya to independent media and human rights monitors, including from international organizations.

37. Ensure that all those held in custody are treated humanely with respect for the inherent dignity of the human person and are held in conditions which at least meet minimum international standards.

38. Make public the names and whereabouts of all persons deprived of their liberty and the charges brought against them, including those detained at border crossings and other checkpoints, in police stations, temporary detention facilities and on the premises of Russian military bases.

39. Take all other measures necessary to prevent "disappearances" including those set out in Amnesty International's 14-Point Program for the Prevention of "Disappearances" (Appendix 3).

40. Ensure full and appropriate access to detainees by the International Committee of the Red Cross.

41. Provide adequate protection and humanitarian assistance, in accordance with principles of humanity and impartiality, to Chechen internally displaced people (IDPs) and other civilians in Chechnya in accordance with the UN Guiding

Principles on Internal Displacement and other applicable international standards. Stop attempts to forcibly return Chechen IDPs back to Chechnya until they can return voluntarily, in safety and with dignity, to their place of origin or choice.

Amnesty International calls on the Chechen armed opposition groups to implement the following recommendations:

42. Take steps to ensure that all fighters fully respect the requirements of international humanitarian law, in particular those protecting civilians and captured combatants.

43. Ensure full and appropriate access to detainees by the International Committee of the Red Cross.

44. Protect and facilitate the operations of any humanitarian agency or human rights organization present in or seeking access to territory under the control of Chechen forces.

International community

Amnesty International calls on the international community to:

45. Expose and condemn human rights violations, such as torture and ill-treatment, committed by Russian law enforcement officials.

46. Condemn human rights abuses and violations of international humanitarian law committed by Russian security forces and Chechen forces in Chechnya.

47. Urge and, if necessary, assist the authorities to ensure that all those responsible for abuses of human rights or international humanitarian law are brought to justice before independent impartial courts established by law and in proceedings which meet international standards of fairness, and take measures to facilitate such proceedings.

48. Put pressure on the Russian authorities vigorously to investigate and prosecute in fair trials the perpetrators of these violations and to abide by their international obligations to promote and protect human rights for everybody.

49. Ensure the enactment of legislation providing for universal jurisdiction over crimes under international law including crimes against humanity; war crimes; genocide; torture,

including rape; "disappearances" and extrajudicial executions, and exercise such jurisdiction whenever cases arise.

50. Ensure that people who have fled the conflict are not returned to Chechnya or other parts of the Russian Federation unless and until their safe and durable return with dignity is assured.

Appendix 1:

12-Point Program for the Prevention of Torture by Agents of the State

(Amnesty International, 1983, 2000)

Torture is a fundamental violation of human rights, condemned by the international community as an offence to human dignity and prohibited in all circumstances under international law. Yet torture persists, daily and across the globe. Immediate steps are needed to confront torture and other cruel, inhuman or degrading treatment or punishment wherever they occur and to eradicate them totally.

Amnesty International calls on all governments to implement the following 12-Point Program for the Prevention of Torture by Agents of the State. It invites concerned individuals and organizations to ensure that they do so. Amnesty International believes that the implementation of these measures is a positive indication of a government's commitment to end torture and to work for its eradication worldwide.

1. Condemn torture

The highest authorities of every country should demonstrate their total opposition to torture. They should condemn torture unreservedly whenever it occurs. They should make clear to all members of the police, military and other security forces that torture will never be tolerated.

2. Ensure access to prisoners

Torture often takes place while prisoners are held incommunicado — unable to contact people outside who could help them or find out what is happening to them. The practice of incommunicado detention should be ended. Governments should ensure that all prisoners are brought before an independent judicial authority without delay after being taken into custody. Prisoners should have access to relatives, lawyers and doctors without delay and regularly thereafter.

3. No secret detention

In some countries torture takes place in secret locations, often after the victims are made to "disappear". Governments should ensure that prisoners are held only in officially recognized places of detention and that accurate information about their arrest and whereabouts is made available immediately to relatives, lawyers and the courts. Effective judicial remedies should be available at all times to enable relatives and lawyers to find out immediately where a prisoner is held and under what authority and to ensure the prisoner's safety.

4. Provide safeguards during detention and interrogation

All prisoners should be immediately informed of their rights. These include the right to lodge complaints about their treatment and to have a judge rule without delay on the lawfulness of their detention. Judges should investigate any evidence of torture and order release if the detention is unlawful. A lawyer should be present during interrogations. Governments should ensure that conditions of detention conform to international standards for the treatment of prisoners and take into account the needs of members of particularly vulnerable groups. The authorities responsible for detention should be separate from those in charge of interrogation. There should be regular, independent, unannounced and unrestricted visits of inspection to all places of detention.

5. Prohibit torture in law

Governments should adopt laws for the prohibition and prevention of torture incorporating the main elements of the UN Convention against Torture and other Cruel, Inhuman or Degrading Treatment or Punishment (Convention against Torture) and other relevant international standards. All judicial and administrative corporal punishments should be abolished. The prohibition of torture and the essential safeguards for its prevention must not be suspended under any circumstances, including states of war or other public emergency.

6. Investigate

All complaints and reports of torture should be promptly, impartially and effectively investigated by a body independent of the alleged perpetrators. The methods and findings of such investigations should be made public. Officials suspected of committing torture should be suspended from active duty during the investigation. Complainants, witnesses and others at risk should be protected from intimidation and reprisals.

7. Prosecute

Those responsible for torture must be brought to justice. This principle should apply wherever alleged torturers happen to be, whatever their nationality or position, regardless of where the crime was committed and the nationality of the victims, and no matter how much time has elapsed since the commission of the crime. Governments must exercise universal jurisdiction over alleged torturers or extradite them, and cooperate with each other in such criminal proceedings. Trials must be fair. An order from a superior officer must never be accepted as a justification for torture.

8. No use of statements extracted under torture

Governments should ensure that statements and other evidence obtained through torture may not be invoked in any proceedings, except against a person accused of torture.

9. Provide effective training

It should be made clear during the training of all officials involved in the custody, interrogation or medical care of prisoners that torture is a criminal act. Officials should be instructed that they have the right and duty to refuse to obey any order to torture.

10. Provide reparation

Victims of torture and their dependants should be entitled to obtain prompt reparation from the state including restitution, fair and adequate financial compensation and appropriate medical care and rehabilitation.

11. Ratify international treaties

All governments should ratify without reservations international treaties containing safeguards against torture, including the UN

Convention against Torture with declarations providing for individual and inter-state complaints. Governments should comply with the recommendations of international bodies and experts on the prevention of torture.

12. Exercise international responsibility

Governments should use all available channels to intercede with the governments of countries where torture is reported. They should ensure that transfers of training and equipment for military, security or police use do not facilitate torture. Governments must not forcibly return a person to a country where he or she risks being tortured.

This 12-Point Program was adopted by Amnesty International in October 2000 as a program of measures to prevent the torture and ill-treatment of people who are in governmental custody or otherwise in the hands of agents of the state. Amnesty International holds governments to their international obligations to prevent and punish torture, whether committed by agents of the state or by other individuals. Amnesty International also opposes torture by armed political groups.

Appendix 2:

14-Point Program for the Prevention of Extrajudicial Executions

(Amnesty International, 1992)

Extrajudicial executions are fundamental violations of human rights and an affront to the conscience of humanity. These unlawful and deliberate killings, carried out by order of a government or with its complicity or acquiescence, have been condemned by the United Nations. Yet extrajudicial executions continue, daily and across the globe.

Many of the victims have been taken into custody or made to "disappear" before being killed. Some are killed in their homes, or in the course of military operations. Some are assassinated by uniformed members of the security forces, or by "death squads" operating with official connivance. Others are killed in peaceful demonstrations.

The accountability of governments for extrajudicial executions is not diminished by the commission of similar abhorrent acts by armed opposition groups. Urgent action is needed to stop extrajudicial executions and bring those responsible to justice.

Amnesty International calls on all governments to implement the following 14-Point Program for the Prevention of Extrajudicial Executions. It invites concerned individuals and organizations to join in promoting the program. Amnesty International believes that the implementation of these measures is a positive indication of a government's commitment to stop extrajudicial executions and to work for their eradication worldwide.

1. Official condemnation

The highest authorities of every country should demonstrate their total opposition to extrajudicial executions. They should make clear to all members of the police, military and other security forces that extrajudicial executions will not be tolerated under any circumstances.

2. Chain-of-command control

Those in charge of the security forces should maintain strict chain-of-command control to ensure that officers under their command do not commit extrajudicial executions. Officials with chain-of-command responsibility who order or tolerate extrajudicial executions by those under their command should be held criminally responsible for these acts.

3. Restraints on use of force

Governments should ensure that law enforcement officials use force only when strictly necessary and only to the minimum extent required under the circumstances. Lethal force should not be used except when strictly unavoidable in order to protect life.

4. Action against 'death squads'

"Death squads", private armies, criminal gangs and paramilitary forces operating outside the chain of command but with official support or acquiescence should be prohibited and disbanded. Members of such groups who have perpetrated extrajudicial executions should be brought to justice.

5. Protection against death threats

Governments should ensure that anyone in danger of extrajudicial execution, including those who receive death threats, is effectively protected.

6. No secret detention

Governments should ensure that prisoners are held only in publicly recognized places of detention and that accurate information about the arrest and detention of any prisoner is made available promptly to relatives, lawyers and the courts. No one should be secretly detained.

7. Access to prisoners

All prisoners should be brought before a judicial authority without delay after being taken into custody. Relatives, lawyers and doctors should have prompt and regular access to them. There should be regular, independent, unannounced and unrestricted visits of inspection to all places of detention.

8. Prohibition in law

Governments should ensure that the commission of an extrajudicial execution is a criminal offence, punishable by sanctions commensurate with the gravity of the practice. The prohibition of extrajudicial executions and the essential safeguards for their prevention must not be suspended under any circumstances, including states of war or other public emergency.

9. Individual responsibility

The prohibition of extrajudicial executions should be reflected in the training of all officials involved in the arrest and custody of prisoners and all officials authorized to use lethal force, and in the instructions issued to them. These officials should be instructed that they have the right and duty to refuse to obey any order to participate in an extrajudicial execution. An order from a superior officer or a public authority must never be invoked as a justification for taking part in an extrajudicial execution.

10. Investigation

Governments should ensure that all complaints and reports of extrajudicial executions are investigated promptly, impartially and effectively by a body which is independent of those allegedly responsible and has the necessary powers and resources to carry out the investigation. The methods and findings of the investigation should be made public. The body of the alleged victim should not be disposed of until an adequate autopsy has been conducted by a suitably qualified doctor who is able to function impartially. Officials suspected of responsibility for extrajudicial executions should be suspended from active duty during the investigation. Relatives of the victim should have access to information relevant to the investigation, should be entitled to appoint their own doctor to carry out or be present at an autopsy, and should be entitled to present evidence. Complainants, witnesses, lawyers, judges and others involved in the investigation should be protected from intimidation and reprisals.

11. Prosecution

Governments should ensure that those responsible for extrajudicial executions are brought to justice. This principle should apply wherever such people happen to be, wherever the crime was committed, whatever the nationality of the perpetrators or victims and no matter how much time has elapsed since the commission of the crime. Trials should be in the civilian courts. The perpetrators should not be allowed to benefit from any legal measures exempting them from criminal prosecution or conviction.

12. Compensation

Dependants of victims of extrajudicial execution should be entitled to obtain fair and adequate redress from the state, including financial compensation.

13. Ratification of human rights treaties and implementation of international standards

All governments should ratify international treaties containing safeguards and remedies against extrajudicial executions, including the International Covenant on Civil and Political Rights and its first Optional Protocol which provides for individual complaints. Governments should ensure full implementation of the relevant provisions of these and other international instruments, including the UN Principles on the Effective Prevention and Investigation of Extra-Legal, Arbitrary and Summary Executions, and comply with the recommendations of intergovernmental organizations concerning these abuses.

14. International responsibility

Governments should use all available channels to intercede with the governments of countries where extrajudicial executions have been reported. They should ensure that training and transfers of equipment, know-how and training for military, security or police use do not facilitate extrajudicial executions. No one should be forcibly returned to a country where he or she risks becoming a victim of extrajudicial execution.

Appendix 3:

14-Point Program for the Prevention of 'Disappearances'

(Amnesty International, 1992)

The "disappeared" are people who have been taken into custody by agents of the state, yet whose whereabouts and fate are concealed, and whose custody is denied. "Disappearances" cause agony for the victims and their relatives. The victims are cut off from the world and placed outside the protection of the law; often they are tortured; many are never seen again. Their relatives are kept in ignorance, unable to find out whether the victims are alive or dead.

The United Nations has condemned "disappearances" as a grave violation of human rights and has said that their systematic practice is of the nature of a crime against humanity. Yet thousands of people "disappear" each year across the globe, and countless others remain "disappeared". Urgent action is needed to stop "disappearances", to clarify the fate of the "disappeared" and to bring those responsible to justice.

Amnesty International calls on all governments to implement the following 14-Point Program for the Prevention of "Disappearances". It invites concerned individuals and organizations to join in promoting the program. Amnesty International believes that the implementation of these measures is a positive indication of a government's commitment to stop "disappearances" and to work for their eradication worldwide.

1. Official condemnation

The highest authorities of every country should demonstrate their total opposition to "disappearances". They should make clear to all members of the police, military and other security forces that "disappearances" will not be tolerated under any circumstances.

2. Chain-of-command control

Those in charge of the security forces should maintain strict chain-of-command control to ensure that officers under their command do not commit "disappearances". Officials with chain-of-command responsibility who order or tolerate "disappearances" by those under their command should be held criminally responsible for these acts.

3. Information on detention and release

Accurate information about the arrest of any person and about his or her place of detention, including transfers and releases, should be made available promptly to relatives, lawyers and the courts. Prisoners should be released in a way that allows reliable verification of their release and ensures their safety.

4. Mechanism for locating and protecting prisoners

Governments should at all times ensure that effective judicial remedies are available which enable relatives and lawyers to find out immediately where a prisoner is held and under what authority, to ensure his or her safety, and to obtain the release of anyone arbitrarily detained.

5. No secret detention

Governments should ensure that prisoners are held only in publicly recognized places of detention. Up-to-date registers of all prisoners should be maintained in every place of detention and centrally. The information in these registers should be made available to relatives, lawyers, judges, official bodies trying to trace people who have been detained, and others with a legitimate interest. No one should be secretly detained.

6. Authorization of arrest and detention

Arrest and detention should be carried out only by officials who are authorized by law to do so. Officials carrying out an arrest should identify themselves to the person arrested and, on demand, to others witnessing the event. Governments should establish rules setting forth which officials are authorized to order an arrest or detention. Any deviation from established procedures which contributes to a "disappearance" should be punished by appropriate sanctions.

7. Access to prisoners

All prisoners should be brought before a judicial authority
without delay after being taken into custody. Relatives, lawyers
and doctors should have prompt and regular access to them.
There should be regular, independent, unannounced and
unrestricted visits of inspection to all places of detention.

8. Prohibition in law

Governments should ensure that the commission of a
"disappearance" is a criminal offence, punishable by sanctions
commensurate with the gravity of the practice. The prohibition
of "disappearances" and the essential safeguards for their
prevention must not be suspended under any circumstances,
including states of war or other public emergency.

9. Individual responsibility

The prohibition of "disappearances" should be reflected in the
training of all officials involved in the arrest and custody of
prisoners and in the instructions issued to them. They should be
instructed that they have the right and duty to refuse to obey
any order to participate in a "disappearance". An order from a
superior officer or a public authority must never be invoked as a
justification for taking part in a "disappearance".

10. Investigation

Governments should ensure that all complaints and reports of
"disappearances" are investigated promptly, impartially and
effectively by a body which is independent of those allegedly
responsible and has the necessary powers and resources to
carry out the investigation. The methods and findings of the
investigation should be made public. Officials suspected of
responsibility for "disappearances" should be suspended from
active duty during the investigation. Relatives of the victim
should have access to information relevant to the investigation
and should be entitled to present evidence. Complainants,
witnesses, lawyers and others involved in the investigation
should be protected from intimidation and reprisals. The
investigation should not be curtailed until the fate of the victim
is officially clarified.

11. Prosecution

Governments should ensure that those responsible for "disappearances" are brought to justice. This principle should apply wherever such people happen to be, wherever the crime was committed, whatever the nationality of the perpetrators or victims and no matter how much time has elapsed since the commission of the crime. Trials should be in the civilian courts. The perpetrators should not benefit from any legal measures exempting them from criminal prosecution or conviction.

12. Compensation and rehabilitation

Victims of "disappearance" and their dependants should be entitled to obtain fair and adequate redress from the state, including financial compensation. Victims who reappear should be provided with appropriate medical care or rehabilitation.

13. Ratification of human rights treaties and implementation of international standards

All governments should ratify international treaties containing safeguards and remedies against "disappearances", including the International Covenant on Civil and Political Rights and its first Optional Protocol which provides for individual complaints. Governments should ensure full implementation of the relevant provisions of these and other international instruments, including the UN Declaration on the Protection of All Persons from Enforced Disappearance, and comply with the recommendations of intergovernmental organizations concerning these abuses.

14. International responsibility

Governments should use all available channels to intercede with the governments of countries where "disappearances" have been reported. They should ensure that transfers of equipment, know-how and training for military, security or police use do not facilitate "disappearances". No one should be forcibly returned to a country where he or she risks being made to "disappear".

Endnotes

1   *Memoirs,* Andrey Sakharov, 1983.

2   *Federal Security Service (FSB) versus prisoner of conscience Aleksandr Nikitin: return to Soviet practices* (AI Index: EUR 46/042/1996).

3   For example, *Torture in Russia: 'This man-made hell'* (AI Index: EUR 46/004/1997).

4   Examples include *For the motherland: Reported grave breaches of international humanitarian law – Persecution of ethnic Chechens in Moscow* (AI Index: EUR 46/046/1999) and *Failure to protect or punish: human rights violations and impunity in Chechnya* (AI Index: EUR 46/004/2002).

5   Small Arms Survey, *'Small Arms Survey 2001 – Profiling the Problem'*, Oxford University Press, 2001. In its 2002 yearbook, the Stockholm International Peace Research Institute (SIPRI) placed Russia as the top arms exporter for 2001 with arms exports worth US$4.97 billion (the USA sold US$4.56 billion worth).

6   *Rosoboronexport* company information 2001.

7   For example, Sudanese forces were reported to have used Russian helicopter gunships to attack civilians at Bieh on 20 February 2002; 17 people were killed. Angola has also been heavily armed by Russia despite the Angolan army's perpetration of human rights violations including deliberately killing prisoners and forcibly removing civilians to areas where food is not available.

8   See OSCE Document on Small Arms and Light Weapons, November 2000.

9   *Rossiiskaia Gazeta,* 3 February 1992.

10   *Russian Federation – savagery begets only savagery* (AI Index: EUR 46/0128/2001).

11   Article 59.

12   However, according to reports, those undertaking alternative service with a university degree may serve for 21 months.

13   Articles 1 and 5 of the International Convention on the Elimination of All Forms of Racial Discrimination.

14   Figure given by Yekaterina Lakhova, head of the Presidential Commission on Women, Children and Demographics as cited in *Radio Free Europe/Radio Liberty Newsline,* Vol. 1, No. 143, Part I, 21 October 1997. See also, Consideration of Reports Submitted by States Parties under Article 18 of the Convention on the Elimination of All Forms of Discrimination against Women, Fifth periodic reports of States Parties, Russian Federation, UN doc CEDAW/C/USR/5, 3 March 1999, part III, B, c (6), p. 38.

15   CEDAW, Consideration of reports of States parties, Russian Federation, fifth report, 28 January 2002; UN doc CEDAW/C/2002/I/CRP.3/Add.3; para. 36.

16   Ibid., para. 37.

17   Concluding Observations of the Committee on the Rights of the Child, Russian Federation, 10 November 1999; UN doc CRC/C/15/Add.110; para. 28.

18   Ibid., para. 68.

19   Ibid., para. 28.

20   Ibid., para. 70.

21   Interview with Aleksei Mikheev conducted by Amnesty International in Nizhnii Novgorod in May 2002.

22   Amnesty International interview with Mara Poliakova, Head of the Council on Legal and Judicial Expertise, July 2001.

23   The investigation was reopened on 19 January 1999 and closed on 25 February 1999 because of lack of evidence. On 1 December 1999 the Nizhnii Novgorod regional procuracy ordered the investigation reopened; this investigation was closed on 24 February 2000 because of lack of evidence. On 16 March 2000 the regional procuracy reopened the investigation, this time ordering the city procuracy to take charge; this investigation was closed on 27 July 2000 because of lack of evidence. On 10 November 2000 the deputy city procurator ordered the case reopened, but the case was closed on 29 December 2000 for the same reason. Aleksei Mikheev appealed to the Nizhnii Novgorod district court, which on 27 March 2001 ordered the city procuracy to reopen the case. This investigation was closed on 19 May 2001. On 7 August 2001 Aleksei Mikheev filed an appeal against this decision with the regional procuracy.

24   *Sledstvennyi izoliator.*

25   The European Committee for the Prevention of Torture and Other Inhuman or Degrading Treatment or Punishment (CPT) has, since 1998, made nine visits to places where people are deprived of their liberty by the Russian authorities. Five of these visits were to Chechnya. The CPT made recommendations to the authorities following each visit aimed at preventing torture and ill-treatment. Regrettably, the Russian authorities, as of mid-2002, had yet to authorize the publication of the reports of the CPT visits, which means that the recommendations to the Russian authorities remain confidential.

26   In May 2002, following the (UN) Committee against Torture's examination of the Russian Federation's periodic report of its implementation of the Convention against Torture, the Committee recommended that the Russian authorities "promptly incorporate into domestic law the definition of torture as contained in Article 1 of the Convention and characterize torture and other cruel, inhuman and degrading treatment as specific crimes with appropriate penalties in domestic law". (UN doc. CAT/C/CR/28/4, para. 8(a), May 2002.)

27   A method of torture involving partial asphyxiation using a gas mask.

28   Letter from Aleksandr Shcherbakov to the Russian non-governmental organization For Human Rights, dated 19 April 2002.

29   From a letter received by Amnesty International from Aleksei Golubkov, 22 March 1999.

30   Aleksei Golubkov was convicted under Article 132 (2) and (3) of the Criminal Code.

31   In May 2002 the Deputy Justice Minister was reported as saying there were 962,000 prisoners in Russia (AFP, 4 May 2002). According to the Moscow office of Penal Reform International, the pre-trial detention population stood at 211,986 on 31 December 2001.

32   See *Torture in Russia: 'This man-made hell'* (AI Index: EUR 46/004/1997).

33 Report of the Special Rapporteur on torture, 16 November 1994; UN doc E/CN.4/1995/34/Add.1; para. 71. His report to the Commission on Human Rights dated 24 December 1997 noted his continuing concern over "torturous conditions of detention in pre-trial detention centres (SIZOs), which appear to persist on a widespread scale despite concrete recommendations he [had] made in the report of his [1994] visit." (UN doc E/CN.4/1998/38, para. 163.)

34 The new CPC places a greater emphasis on alternatives to pre-trial detention than its predecessor.

35 Report presented to the Russian President and the Federal Assembly on 29 April 2002 by the Procurator-General, as reported by the BBC, 5 May 2002.

36 AFP, 4 May 2002.

37 "Women in Russian Prisons", *Sbornik materialov 2001*, Moscow Centre for Penal Reform, p. 6.

38 9th General Report on the CPT's activities covering the period 1 January to 31 December 1998, Ref: CPT/Inf(99) 12[Eng], para 30, 30 August 1999.

39 Amnesty International interviewed Marina T. (pseudonym) in May 2002.

40 Rule 53 of the UN Standard Minimum Rules for the Treatment of Prisoners states that "Women prisoners shall be attended and supervised only by women officers". The CPT has regularly recommended that "persons detained by the police should be entitled to have a lawyer present during any interrogation conducted by the police (whether this be during or after the initial period of police custody).

41 UN Doc. CEDAW/C/2002/I/CRP.3/Add.3; para. 38 (Concluding Observations/Comments).

42 In Russian, *Vytrezvitel* — these are official facilities operated by the Interior Ministry to which people suspected of being drunk are taken and held until they are sober.

43 Both Sergei Kalinin (pseudonym) and his mother, whom Amnesty International interviewed in Moscow on 29 May 2002, requested anonymity fearing reprisals from the police.

44 Committee on the Rights of the Child, Concluding Observations following consideration of the reports of states parties, Russian Federation, second periodic report, 10 November 1999. UN Doc. CRC/C/15/Add.110, para 28.

45 In Russian law, a juvenile is anyone aged 18 or under.

46 In an address to the Russian *Duma*, the Procurator-General stated that 1.14 million juveniles were charged by police (as reported in the *Moscow Times*, 21 February 2002). According to the Procurator-General's annual report, juvenile crime constituted almost a 10th of all crimes committed in Russia in 2001, as reported by the internet news site http://www.strana.ru

47 Article 122 of the old CPC requires the police to inform the procurator within 24 hours of a person's detention.

48 In addition, educational provision to juveniles in SIZOs is reported to be inadequate. According to Liudmila Al'pern of the Moscow Centre for Penal Reform (interviewed in mid-2002), instead of holding classes, teachers visit detained juveniles in their cells.

49 The Parliamentary Assembly of the Council of Europe noted earlier this year that "the Russian federal authorities have achieved notable progress in abolishing the remains of the old propiska (internal registration) system". However, the Assembly regretted "that restrictive registration requirements continue to be enforced, often in a discriminatory manner, against ethnic minorities. Therefore, the Assembly reiterates its call made in Recommendation 1544 (2001), in which it urged member states concerned 'to undertake a thorough review of national laws and policies with a view to eliminating any provisions which might impede the right to freedom of movement and choice of place of residence within internal borders'"; Resolution 1277 (2002), para 8, xii; text adopted by the Parliamentary Assembly on 23 April 2002 (11th sitting).

50 See Second Report on the Russian Federation of the European Commission against Racism and Intolerance, adopted March 2001; Ref: CRI(2001)41, para. 79.

51 *Regional'noe upravlenie po bor'be s organizovannoi prestupnost'iu* — the Regional Department on fighting Organized Crime, or Organized Crime Squad.

52 Sources of information for this case include Memorial, an interview with the lawyer, Inna Ailamazian, and an article in *Obshchaya Gazeta*, 21/27 March 2002.

53 See, in particular, Principle 24 of this body of principles.

54 Article 58 of the old CPC contained a similar provision.

55 In Russian, *mery presechenia.*

56 Article 9(3) of the ICCPR.

57 The new CPC prohibits cases from being sent for further investigation in these circumstances.

58 Letter received on 7 March 2002 by the Russian human rights organization, the Committee for Civil Rights.

59 On 18 December 2001 a Butyrskii district court found Tigran Airapetian guilty of extortion but, as he qualified under an amnesty, took no further measures against him.

60 *Combatting Torture in Europe* by Rod Morgan and Malcolm Evans, p. 76 and fn 34.

61 For example, Article 14(1) of the Convention against Torture.

62 In Russian, *Federalnaia sluzhba bezopasnosti,* the state security service and successor agency to the KGB or *Komitet gosudarstvennoi bezopasnosti.*

63 *Vremennoe otdelenie vnutrennikh del* — temporary police station.

64 On 9 January 2001, for example, armed men believed to be under the command of one of the principal commanders of the Chechen forces, kidnapped *Médecins Sans Frontières* aid worker Kenneth Gluck near the village of Starye Atagi. He was released without payment of a ransom three weeks later.

65 In April 2000 Chechen fighters claimed to have executed nine OMON members from the Russian city of Perm whom they had captured in combat; see Elizabeth Piper, "Rebels Say They Executed 9 OMON", *The Moscow Times*, 6 April 2000.

66 In December 1999 the Russian Federal Migration Service issued Order no. 110 to the Regional Migration Services of north Caucasus republics to stop that body registering new arrivals. In Ingushetia, this order has been implemented

sporadically. See *UNHCR Paper on Asylum Seekers from the Russian Federation in the context of the situation in Chechnya,* January 2002, para. 28.

67 Estimates put the number of fatalities between 20,000 and 80,000.

68 See, generally, Romanas Sedlickas and Stasys Knezys, *The War in Chechnya,* Texas A&M University Press, September 1999.

69 See, Organization for Security and Co-operation in Europe *Annual Report 1997 on OSCE Activities,* 18 December 1997, p. 15, para. 2.2.2.

70 According to the human rights organization Memorial, up to 144 civilians were killed; see report by Memorial, *By All Available Means,* available online at: http://www.memo.ru/hr/hotpoints/chechen/samashki/engl/

71 See "Chechnya Converts to Islam", *The Moscow Times,* 10 June 1997.

72 No armed group has claimed responsibility for these attacks.

73 During the trial, the prosecution alleged the men were carrying out the orders of a Chechen warlord. The court ignored claims by the men that their confessions had been extracted under torture; see, Nabi Abdulayev, "Six Convicted in Bombing of Apartment Building", *Associated Press,* 19 March 2001.

74 See for example the ruling of the International Criminal Tribunal for the former Yugoslavia, *Prosecutor v. Blaskic, Decision on the Defence Motion to Strike Portions of the Amended Indictment Alleging "Failure to Punish" Liability,* 4 April 1997, para. 10.

75 (UN) Commission on Human Rights resolution 2000/58, adopted on 25 April 2000 and (UN) Commission on Human Rights resolution 2001/24, adopted on 20 April 2001.

76 The Russian Federation has agreed to visits by three mechanisms: the Special Rapporteur on violence against women, its causes and consequences, the Special Representative of the Secretary-General for Children and Armed Conflict and the Special Representative of the Secretary General on Internally Displaced Persons. However, invitations have yet to be extended to the Special Rapporteur on extrajudicial, summary or arbitrary executions and the Special Rapporteur on torture.

77 For example, the Russian government attacked a resolution passed in April 2001 by the UN Commission on Human Rights which strongly condemned human rights abuses by Russian forces in Chechnya, and declared that it would not comply with the demands set out in the resolution. The international community failed to pursue actively implementation of these or previous recommendations.

78 Recommendation of the Commissioner for Human Rights "Concerning certain rights that must be guaranteed during the arrest and detention of persons following 'cleansing' operations in the Chechen Republic of the Russian Federation", CommDH/Rec 2002), 30 May 2002; see also, generally, Parliamentary Assembly resolutions on the Chechnya conflict including Resolution 1227 (September 2000), Resolution 1240 (January 2001) and Resolution 1270 (2002) available online at http://assembly.coe.int

79 Conflict in Chechnya – Implementation by Russia of Recommendation 1444 (2000), Doc. 8697, report by Lord Judd on behalf of the Political Affairs Committee of the Parliamentary Assembly of the Council of Europe, 4 April 2000, para. 18.

80 Ibid., para. 18

81 See, for example, Amnesty International press release, *Chechnya: Civilians stranded in Grozny must be allowed to escape bombing* (AI Index: EUR 46/002/2000), 12 January 2000.

82 Russian authorities have claimed in 2002 that there are no longer such operations as *zachistka*. Rather, they claim that they conduct passport checks of residents in Chechnya or targeted operations.

83 In November 2001 Amnesty International delegates travelled to neighbouring Ingushetia to interview victims and witnesses to violations including torture, "disappearances" and extrajudicial executions. See, for example, *Russian Federation: Failure to protect or punish: human rights violations and impunity in Chechnya* (AI Index: EUR 46/004/2002).

84 In Russian, *Otriad militsii osobogo naznachenia*, special police detachments or riot police.

85 In Russian, *kontraktniki*.

86 These injuries were confirmed by a medical examination by a *Médecins Sans Frontières* doctor in Nazran, Ingushetia, on 13 July 2001.

87 In a public statement issued in July 2001 the CPT indicated that "a considerable number of people deprived of their liberty in the Chechen Republic since the outset of the conflict had been physically ill-treated by members of Russian armed forces or law enforcement agencies." It said that during the CPT's visit in March 2001, it once again received "numerous credible and consistent allegations... of severe ill-treatment by Russian Federal forces". The CPT issued this statement as an extraordinary measure as a result of its view that its dialogue with the Russian authorities on issues related to torture and ill-treatment and impunity in Chechnya had "reached an impasse". (CPT/inf 2001) 15).

88 A number of people from the village of Kurcheloi reported this case to Amnesty International.

89 Amnesty International interviewed Zaindi Bisultanoi in November 2001.

90 See, for example, Human Rights Watch, *Russia/Chechnya: February 5: A Day of Slaughter in Novye Aldi*, vol. 12 no. 9, June 2000.

91 On 4 June 2001, Special Representative to the President of the Russian Federation on Chechnya, Vladimir Kalamanov, reportedly stated that over 540 Chechens had gone missing without trace since the beginning of the conflict; see, Amelia Gentleman, "Kremlin Admits Hundreds Missing in Chechnya", *The Guardian*, 5 June 2001.

92 See Human Rights Watch, *Last Seen....: Continued "disappearances" in Chechnya*, April 2002.

93 Article 1(2) of the UN Declaration on the Protection of All Persons from Enforced Disappearance, states that: "Any act of enforced disappearance places the persons subjected thereto outside the protection of the law and inflicts severe suffering on them and their families."

94 See the record of a meeting held on 12 January 2002 between Russian government officials, including the procurator for Chechnya, Vsevolod Chernov, and the special representative for Chechnya, Vladimir Kalamanov, and Russian

human rights groups, including Memorial, available online in Russian at
http://www.memo.ru/hr/hotpoints/northkavkaz.htm

95 At the time of writing the case was ongoing.

96 See, Simon Saradzhyan, "Colonel on Trial for Chechen Murder", *The Moscow Times*, 1 March 2001, p.1.

97 Report by Alvaro Gil-Robles, Commissioner for Human Rights of the Council of Europe, on his visit to the Russian Federation and the Republic of Chechnya, CommDH (2001) 3, 14 March 2001, Section IV, para. 6.

98 On 1 and 26 March 2002, in response to appeals from members of Amnesty International's Urgent Action network, the main military procuracy wrote to Amnesty International stating that the appeals on the case had been forwarded to the North Caucasus procuracy. The letter stated that the North Caucasus procuracy would inform Amnesty International of any developments in the case. As of July 2002, there had been no further information on the status of any investigation into the "disappearance" of Aset Yakhiaeva and Milana Betirgirieva.

99 UN Doc: E/CN.4/2001/73, para. 103.

100 Cited in Maura Reynolds, "Troops Still Abusing Chechens Russian Says", *Los Angeles Times*, 21 May 2002.

101 See *Russian Federation: Failure to protect or punish – human rights violations and impunity in Chechnya* (AI Index: EUR 46/004/2002).

102 Interviewed by Amnesty International in Ingushetia in March 2000.

103 CPT Inf (2001) 15, 10 July 2001.

104 See *Report on the activities of the Joint Working Group (JWG) on Chechnya made up of members of the Parliamentary Assembly of the Council of Europe and of the State Duma of the Federal Assembly of the Russian Federation*, Addendum 1 to the Progress Report, presented by Lord Judd and Mr. Dmitri Rogozin, co-chairmen of the JWG, Doc. 9415. The Parliamentary Assembly of the Council of Europe decided to establish the JWG in January 2001. (See Resolution 1240 (2001) on the conflict in the Chechen Republic – recent developments.)